THE CHAIRMAN'S GUIDE

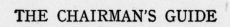

THE

CHAIRMAN'S GUIDE

AND

SECRETARY'S COMPANION

WITH USEFUL HINTS FOR THE
CONDUCT OF BUSINESS AND
SOCIAL GATHERINGS OF ALL
KINDS

WARD, LOCK & CO., LIMITED
LONDON AND MELBOURNE

MADE IN ENGLAND

PRINTED IN GREAT BRITAIN BY PURNELL AND SONS, LTD.
PAULTON (SOMERSET) AND LONDON

PREFACE

The Chairman's Guide and Secretary's Companion has for
a generation been accepted as a standard authority. It is
in use as a text-book at Business Colleges, and it forms part
of the office equipment of public companies. In private
life it is the silent mentor of innumerable persons called to
the chair at political or social gatherings or who, in great-
hearted ignorance, have shouldered the responsibilities of
an honorary secretaryship. And always the *Chairman's
Guide* has proved equal to the occasion. Why then, it may
be asked, make alterations ? The answer is that conditions
change, and handbooks must move with the times.

But improvement cannot stop with the bringing up to
date of the various sections, especially the legal references.
The conquests of our previous editions have brought into
view new fields to be occupied. Particularly is this true
about secretarial work. The Secretary's Companion, therefore, has been greatly extended and now covers the whole
field, including in its survey the secretary employee of a
great company with an office staff under his control and the
independent secretary of several small concerns for whom he
supplies registered office and board room. Included in the
additions to the Chairman section is a suggested set of rules
to govern meetings for which the standard rules derived from
Parliamentary procedure have never really been applicable
and which, on this account, often lapse into lawlessness.
This and much else has been added without any sacrifice of
the old well-tried and popular features.

Every phase of Public Procedure so far as the chairman
is concerned is discussed in these pages. This includes the
Election and duties of a Chairman ; the routine to be followed

at General Meetings of Companies and other Bodies; the
Regulations as to Quorum and other matters pertaining to
the constitution of a Meeting, with some consideration of
the Minutes; the important and in certain respects intricate
questions involved in Motions and Amendments submitted
for debate, with careful elucidation of particular Motions,
such as those for Adjournment and the "Previous Question";
an account of several peculiarities in Parliamentary procedure; illustrations of the various types of "orderly" Amendments; an exposition of the relations between Chairman and
Members; an explanation of the duties of the Chairman at
social functions; and a description of the Chairman's work
in Committee. Included also is an unique chapter on the
Conduct and Control of the Chairman at a Meeting where
disorder is threatened or is in progress, the text being based
on information not readily accessible. The chapter containing several pattern speeches which may be utilised either
actually (with the necessary modifications to suit time, place,
and circumstance), or as models on which chairmen may
prefer to work up their own remarks, will be found distinctly
helpful. In another chapter suggestions are offered as to the
qualities, or "points," which should be looked for in making
choice of a chairman. Considerable space is devoted to a
statement of the practice of the London County Council, so
far as it affects the chairman, founded upon the elaborate
and valuable Standing Orders of that body.

Most of the text has been derived from prolonged personal
experience of attendance—sometimes as chairman, sometimes
as secretary, and sometimes as one of the audience—at
meetings of various descriptions; but the writer has con-
sulted, and has been greatly indebted to, the standard
authorities, more especially the "Parliamentary Practice"
of Lord Farnborough (still, perhaps, better known to some
readers by his earlier name of Sir Thomas Erskine May),
Sir Reginald Palgrave's "Chairman's Handbook," and Sir
Francis Beaufort Palmer's "Company Law."

CONTENTS

CONTENTS

CONTENTS

THE SECRETARY'S COMPANION

CONTENTS

THE CHAIRMAN'S GUIDE

CHAPTER I

ELECTING A CHAIRMAN.

False Alarms.—For reasons that often are quite insufficient, most men and women are afraid to let themselves be nominated for the position of chairman, whether of a public meeting, a social gathering, or even of a committee. Partly this is because they exaggerate the difficulties of the office. On this point we can reassure them. There is no reason why any man or woman of equable disposition and ordinary sagacity should not fill the post. It is true that more than this should be sought in a chairman (see Chapter XIV. "The Choice of a Chairman"); but people can't always find what they seek, and the fact that a particular person is offered the position, or a nomination for it, suggests that he is as well qualified to fill it as anyone in sight. Self-distrust arises also from a consciousness of ignorance of procedure; but this defect can be remedied quite easily by a study of our hand-book.

Election of Chairman.—We may now proceed to consider the election of a chairman, whether he is chosen for the meeting only, or for the year. The period for which chairmen are appointed to preside over the deliberations of County Councils, Education Committees, Municipal Boards, Boards of Directors of Railways or Companies, and the like, is regulated generally by Act of Parliament, the Standing Orders of public bodies, Articles of Association, or, in less important cases, simply by usage and choice of those assembled.

Chairmen of Town Councils or Education Committees are elected for varying periods; of Municipal Boards, and such-like offices, commonly for one year; Chairmen of Companies, etc., in accordance with the Articles of Association, and of Ordinary Meetings for the duration of the meeting.

Choice of Chairman.—At the first occasion when any members meet to choose a chairman, it is supposed that the majority present have made themselves acquainted with the most fitting person for this office. Perhaps the members present may have agreed tacitly upon the person who shall be chairman, and then, as soon as one of their number nominates him, the assent of the meeting is given in a manner practically unanimous. This method is the simplest, and the person so elected takes his seat accordingly.

Temporary Chairman.—If, however, the nomination is objected to, and another name, or more than one, is put forward, a temporary chairman—of course, one not in the running—should be voted into the chair, in order to conduct the proceedings. In the case of conspicuous bodies, such as the London County Council, the rule is that the chairman of the year continues in power until his successor has accepted office and is ready to preside.

Candidate's Opportunity.—The person first nominated has now an excellent opportunity to show his fitness for the position he seeks to fill. He should display no disappointment or irritation at the perhaps unlooked-for appearance of rivals. Each candidate may believe himself the best fitted for the office. But the opinion of the Assembly is the crucial test.

Proposers of Temporary Chairman.—The temporary chairman is usually proposed by the conveners of the meeting. This is the fair procedure, and is the common-sense rule. They will doubtless elect a proper person for such business. Those who have called the meeting will be most likely to understand the various requirements for its conduct, and in all likelihood are prepared with a temporary occupant of the chair. This is, indeed, essential to avoid sheer waste of time.

The person elected is then conducted, as the temporary ruler of the meeting, to the chair. He assumes the reins at once, beginning by calling on a nominator to propose a candidate, and intimating that only a few minutes (say, three) will be allowed for speech. This the proposer does as in Parliamentary procedure, addressing the chair, and is entitled to "the floor" until his time is up. It is quite unusual to see a contest for the chairmanship of an ordinary business or social meeting, as this is ordinarily settled beforehand.

Nominees should be Present.—The chairman nominated must be present at the meeting when his name is proposed. The first speaker, having nominated his candidate, moves that the said nominee "do take the chair." This must be submitted formally to the meeting as a motion—viz., "That Mr. —— do take the chair."

The Motion and Procedure.—The next step is to second the motion, and when this has been done—should no other candidate be proposed—the chairman will put it forthwith, saying in effect that "the question before the meeting, moved by Mr. F. and seconded by Mr. G., is, that" etc., etc.

Voting.—On this he will take the sense of the meeting. This he must do even when he is aware that the election will not be opposed, for should this form not be observed, it is obvious that the later proceedings might be invalidated. The customary method of voting is by a show of hands.

No Seconder.—Should the mover find no one to second his motion, it drops, and another name is introduced. Accordingly, the name of the next candidate upon the list is brought forward, and the same method of procedure is employed.

Discussion Strictly Limited.—The temporary chairman must rigidly confine the proposers of several candidates to a time limit. All that is requisite is a few sentences setting forth the qualifications of each man for the post, and for this three minutes is ample. Speaking must be limited to the proposer only.

Procedure.—Where more than one name is proposed it is the rule to put up each name as a candidate *per se*, not as an "amendment" upon the previous nomination. This is only courteous, as each candidate is entitled to identical consideration and treatment by the temporary chairman, and should receive it. As soon as every candidate has been duly proposed and seconded, the temporary chairman will immediately proceed with the voting. The audience must be anxious to get to business, and have made up their minds whom they mean to support. Accordingly the first name upon the list, which will contain the names in the order in which they were proposed, is submitted to the meeting in the usual form of Question—viz., "That Mr. —— do take the chair." The voting upon this is by a show of hands. Should the "Noes" have it, a record must be taken of the number of "Ayes" (for a reason that will appear), and the second name on the list put to the meeting. If no nomination is carried, it is the usual procedure at what may be called isolated meetings to call to the chair the candidate who has received the largest number of votes. This is permissible and often advisable. The chairman's occupancy of the position may be for only a couple of hours, all told. People called together to consider some particular subject are rightly impatient to get to it, and intolerant of delay on formalities. But the election of a chairman for a year, or even of a temporary chairman in certain circumstances, is no mere formality—it can be of vital importance. Here, to ascertain the real choice of the meeting, something is demanded more accurate in its working than the rough-and-ready method just described. How unfairly this might work a little reflection will show. A., with only fifteen "ayes" to B.'s sixteen, might be everyone's second choice, whereas "B." might be absolutely obnoxious to the great majority. This might easily happen if he were advocating some departure generally distrusted. The little clique that voted for him might be more numerous than the supporters of any other single candidate. To prevent such misrepresentation the following procedure is recommended. The name that has secured the smallest number of votes is struck out and the remaining names are put to the meeting as before. If no majority appears, the lowest candidate in the second election is eliminated, and the process is repeated until some one gets a majority or only one name is left, which is the choice of the meeting. Usually a result is reached long before the list has been whittled down to one.

Although the process of elimination is the most accurate way of arriving at the mind of the meeting when no candidate at the first vote gets an absolute majority, it is not essential. A chairman can be duly elected by the "rough-and ready" procedure described on page 18 or by a ballot which has placed him at the top but in a minority of the total votes polled. But in this matter, as in others, if the company or assembly has a rule, it must be followed.

Putting a Motion.—The chairman should be careful when putting any motion to remember that motions always begin with the word "That."

Decision by Lot.—The chairman has power to decide "by lot" the choice of a candidate if two nominees have an equal number of votes. Indeed, an Act of Parliament legalised this procedure. But no chairman in these days would dream of exercising this method of choice. Should hands be equal, he has a better expedient in the casting vote.

Casting Vote.—A casting vote may be given by the temporary occupant of the chair, and therefore care should be exercised as to the person elected to fill the office *pro tem.* It is unusual, but it may happen, that the temporary occupant of the chair is so highly esteemed and otherwise so popular that he is invited to assume the permanent tenure by general consent.

CHAPTER II

DUTIES OF A CHAIRMAN.

HAVING now secured our chairman, the temporary occupant leaves the chair after some one has, for courtesy's sake, proposed a vote of thanks, and this has been accorded to him for his services.

The Chairman in the Chair.—The chairman is then escorted to the chair, and in some assemblies is formally introduced to the meeting by one of the seniors. He then thanks the audience, and assumes his position.

His Fitness for the Post.—Now the measure of fitness of the man for his position will be perceived, and, indeed, it is to be hoped that his suitability has been evident before. Calmness and impartiality will be at once recognised, while any nervous uncertainty will be as quickly commented upon; though a "new hand," otherwise competent, may count upon the indulgence of his colleagues until he gets into his stride. The chairman's duties are to maintain order, to hold the reins, and, as it were, "feel the mouth" of the meeting. He must not drive furiously, but gently, and keep his hands upon the bridle and the curb. Good temper, tact, courtesy, and firmness are essential to the occupant of the chair. To possess the respect of the audience is to lead it.

The Chairman's Eye.—Apart from custom in local self-governing bodies, where the spokesmen are usually readily distinguished—the chairman's practice being to select from members on their feet a speaker from each side alternately—an important duty of the chairman may be to fix upon the proper and the most suitable speakers in a debate or discussion. The knack of seeing and non-seeing may be practised with much success, and greatly to the advantage of a debate, by a judicious chairman, or by the "Speaker" in Parliament.

It need scarcely be explained that meetings of this description are few and far between, being almost exclusively confined to local Parliaments, in which House of Commons procedure is somewhat slavishly followed. The chairman of an assembly of this kind, therefore, is not likely to need very much "coaching."

His Position.—The chairman is, of course, upon a raised seat, so placed that he can command the meeting. He is supposed to be separated from every influence for or against any topic or question. He should in his private capacity communicate on municipal or council business with no one save the clerk, secretary, or other office-bearer, and should strive to put all feeling of sympathy aside, and avoid suspicion of favouritism or advocacy. This is very important.

Respect Due to Him.—The chairman being seated, and finding the meeting ready, rises and demands silence. If need be, attention should be called to his rising by cries of "Chair! Chair!" and silence should immediately be observed. If it is not, the chairman should call for it.

Opening the Proceedings.—The chairman, having first called upon the secretary to read (or having himself read) the notice convening the meeting, may then briefly and succinctly address the assembly, explaining its object. Having thus put everyone in possession of the *raison d'être* of the gathering, he will call upon some person to speak to the question, naming the person audibly, so that the audience may know who is about to speak. In exceptional cases an agreed rotation of speakers may have been determined beforehand, but generally speaking (and always in public meetings), anyone may rise to speak after a resolution has been moved and seconded. In such event the chairman will require the speaker's name, so that he may announce it to the gathering.

Reading of Minutes.—But when there are minutes to be read, the first proceeding is to call upon the secretary to read them. In meetings which take place with certain regularity, such as committee meetings, etc., the reading of the minutes of the previous meeting is the first item upon the agenda.

The chairman having obtained silence, calls upon the secretary accordingly, and he reads the minutes of the last meeting. This done, the chairman asks the meeting (or committee) whether these correctly represent the transactions at the last meeting; if so, they will signify the same in the usual manner. The only point which can arise on the minutes is whether the record of this or that transaction is correct or not, and the chairman must on no account permit any other discussion of the minutes.

If assented to, the chairman signs them. If an alteration is suggested, and approved, the needed amendment is made and initialled before the minutes are passed. It should be remembered that every alteration of a minute must be initialled by the clerk or secretary.

General Business of the Meeting.—The general business according to the agenda is then proceeded with. The chairman will call upon the first speaker, either selecting him, or permitting him to rise voluntarily. In any case, as we have already said, he should announce him to the meeting.

Of Speaking of Members.—It may happen that two or more of those present may wish to address the chair. In such a case the chairman may choose the speaker. Here his tact and acumen will be tested. If he does not select the most desirable speaker, there may be dissent among the audience, which may call for another.

In the House of Commons Mr. Speaker is omnipotent. He rules completely, and the member who catches not the Speaker's Eye may fume and languish until such other time as the traditional Eye beams upon him.

But in General Meetings a cry may arise for a certain speaker to be heard, and even a motion may be advanced by someone, and seconded, "That Mr. Smith be heard." If such a proposition is made, and formally seconded, the chairman must put the question to the meeting, without further debate, in the usual form, "That," etc.

Motion to Hear a Speaker.—If the motion is carried, Mr. Smith rises, and the chairman's nominee retires, at any rate for the time being; but if the motion is rejected the person originally called upon will open his speech. It is, however, an extreme proceeding on the part of an audience to interfere thus peremptorily with a speaker who has caught the chairman's eye, and the latter may avert ill-feeling by intimating that he will call upon the audience's nominee next.

Debate.—During the debate or meeting the chairman must put down firmly but courteously any appearance of disorder. Now and again a meeting may, unless held well in hand, degenerate into a brawl in which everyone tries to speak at once, and where personalities are, as a consequence, often exchanged.

Checking Misbehaviour.—Any tendency to such behaviour must be promptly and sternly repressed by the authority of the chair, and if persisted in, the chairman may declare the meeting closed. All discussion, therefore, which has no actual bearing upon the question before the meeting, should be stopped; but, if permitted, must be formulated. Often an audience anticipates irrelevancy by loud and persistent cries of "Question! Question!" These symptoms should put the chairman on the *qui vive.*

The Form of Motion.—The chairman should request the speaker to put his views in concluding into the crystallised form of a motion, which will then, if in order, be seconded, and come before the meeting for adoption or rejection. Strictly speaking, such motion should be handed up to the chairman in writing, and he should invariably require this to be done. The next speaker must be someone in sympathy with the first, his speech taking the form of a seconding of the motion. After that the subject is open for general discussion. Although it is convenient that ayes and noes should alternate, and the chairman may try to secure this, his guidance must be persuasive only. But he can be authoritative in making speakers keep to the point and must rule and maintain that no discussion, save upon the motion, is permissible. No person can address the meeting upon a motion until it has been seconded, either formally or fully. If no seconder is found, the motion cannot be proceeded with.

With regard to amendments, the same practice usually obtains, but not necessarily. The need for a seconder to an amendment is not recognized by law. Unless the regulations otherwise provide, an amendment need not be seconded if put and voted on (see Chapter on amendments, p. 61). A person may second a motion formally by raising his hat, or his hand, or by nodding, and does not thereby forfeit his right of speech at a later period of the debate, should he care to exercise it. The seconder of an amendment has not this privilege.

If no amendment is moved and seconded, the motion will be put to the meeting. Save in Parliamentary practice (which in this case has been replaced by the common sense of many meetings), an amendment shall be put to the vote *before* the motion to which it refers and, should it be carried, it will then become itself the substantive motion and when put, as such, another amendment may be proposed to it.

Impersonality of the Chairman.—Throughout the proceedings it is necessary to insist that the chairman shall be impersonal. He is only Mr. Chairman, and must be so addressed, the speaker standing. All other persons should remain seated and silent. If not, the chairman should call them to order, and firmly discountenance any interruptions if the meeting have elected to hear the speaker. But if the man is a bore, or strongly objectionable to the great majority, and if, after an appeal in his favour from the chair, the disturbance continues, then, should it be brought forward, the chairman must accept from the meeting a duly moved and seconded motion "That Mr. —— be no longer heard." This must be put at once and without debate.

" That the Question be now Put."—All partial and irrelevant interruption must be crushed; but if a person rises and the meeting declines to hear him and business threatens to be brought to a standstill, then, unless the obnoxious person gives way, the chairman has no option but to leave the chair and adjourn the meeting where his authority is disregarded, unless someone in the audience shall have moved

and another seconded, and it be carried "that the question be now put"—or "postponed" or "adjourned."

The chairman may insist upon the removal of the offender or offenders if the obstruction is deliberate and confined to one or two persons only. Order must be preserved, and the general sense of the meeting will support the chair. The chairman must, however, listen to any motion made by an obnoxious speaker, if he conducts himself with propriety, and this motion must be brought forward, no matter how unpalatable to some, if it is in order and within the bounds of the objects of the meeting. It may not be seconded, in which case it will drop.

The Question of Order.—The chairman must not put any motion that is out of order, and anything which is not relevant to the objects of the meeting *is* out of order. That is why the chairman, or someone on his behalf, sometimes considers it wise at the very start to read the notice calling the meeting, or to explain the objects of it in a brief preparatory speech. Anything studiously offensive, or any motion dealing with subjects that have already been discussed and voted upon, is out of order. In the latter case, some member is likely to direct attention to the point. In this matter great powers rest with the chairman, who can, on his own initiative, rule that a proposition is out of order, and he should not hesitate to use them. Of course, no chairman worthy of the name would rule as out of order a motion which was not actually open to this charge.

One Man, One Speech.—When a motion is before the meeting it is permissible for members present to speak for or against it. But no person shall speak to it a second time, unless to correct some error of his own, or of a later speaker, or to answer a question asked in debate.

A member who has spoken to a motion cannot move an amendment but can afterwards speak to an amendment that another person has proposed.

Right of Reply.—The proposer of a motion, however, has a right of reply, but this must be strictly confined to points raised in the debate, and must not introduce any fresh matter. No other person whatever possesses any right of reply, and the chairman must be deaf to all appeals, however pathetic, even "for a little one." It may seem hard, but it is better to give the chairman no discretion in such matters, rather than risk the imputation of favouritism, and perhaps open for a second time the floodgates of debate. As already said, an explanation may be allowed, or a repudiation of an argument erroneously ascribed to a speaker, but beyond this the rule must not be relaxed.

Putting the Question.—The mover of the resolution having exercised his "right of reply," as it is termed, or having waived it, the chairman shall close the debate by putting the question to the meeting and obtaining the votes. If a poll is demanded, the tellers (whom the chairman shall nominate before taking the poll) count the ayes and the noes, and hand the result to the chairman, who will declare the numbers for and against the motion, and declare it carried or lost.

Casting Vote.—Then the question of the chairman's vote comes in. Not only does he possess a vote, but he may use his vote and give a casting vote besides, as we have already mentioned. This practice has become customary in all public bodies. He may even give his first, or deliberate vote, in one way, and his second, or casting vote, in another; but he must be chary of such contrariety. Common law gives the chairman no casting vote. This means that where there is no statute law on the point the chairman has no right to a second vote. But there *is* statute law for limited companies and by this the chairman is expressly given a casting vote (Article 52, Table A in the first Schedule to the Companies Act, 1929). Companies are not obliged to follow these articles; they are allowed to register articles of their own. If a company's articles confer (as they generally do) a second vote on the chairman, that settles it. Public administrative bodies, county and town councils and the like have their procedure fixed by law. Common law, practically, has a very restricted authority where meetings are concerned.

The Old Point of View.—It used to be thought that to give a chairman the right to his deliberative vote was to give him undue influence; but later experience has admitted that it is unreasonable to require a man to occupy the chair and at the same time forfeit his undoubted right to express his own opinion.

Reason for the Change.—Practically, the chairman never votes unless on very crucial questions, or in the event of an equality of votes. It is, as a rule, quite exceptional to find anyone disposed, intentionally or otherwise, to abuse his position and power. By the necessity of the case, neither the Speaker nor the Chairman of Committee in the House of Commons has a deliberative vote, but both may be called upon to exercise a casting vote.

The Chairman and the Tie.—It need not be said that no chairman will give a casting vote lightly. When, however, he holds strong, reasoned views on the question at issue he may, in such circumstance, vote in accordance with his own convictions. In the case of a tie vote on an amendment, it has been held that he ought to vote against the amendment on the ground that, as the numbers are equal and a preponderance in favour of the amendment has not been shown, the original motion may be deemed to "hold the field." But it is impossible to lay down hard-and-fast regulations, although there is something to be said on behalf of the view just enunciated. At the same time even supposing the chairman had voted for the amendment and so caused it to be carried, the debate need not be considered as closed, since, as we have seen, the amendment must itself be again put as a substantive motion, and so opportunity is afforded for another amendment to it, which may enable further light to be cast upon the subject.

Points of Detail.—The foregoing are the general duties of a chairman in his office at meetings. But there are many details to be considered, many side-lights to be thrown upon procedure, and upon general business. "Motions and Withdrawals," "Amendments," "Closure" and "Polls and Proxies" are given separate chapters.

Chairman Absent.—There is one point, however, which must not be omitted, even from this first general survey— viz., the accident of the appointed chairman's absence. It may happen that the usual chairman is detained, or unexpectedly prevented from attending. His non-appearance must be met as follows: If there is a vice- or a deputy-chairman there is no difficulty, as it is unlikely that both of them will also be absent. After waiting a few minutes, in the absence of any information regarding the chairman, the vice- or the deputy-chairman will occupy the chair—the former having the prior claim—and proceed to business in the usual manner. If no vice- or deputy-chairman is present a chairman is elected as described on pages 16 and 17.

Waiting is not compulsory in the absence of any special regulation to the contrary. Business may be entered upon immediately the time fixed for beginning the proceedings has arrived. But as a matter of courtesy a few minutes' "law" is allowed. The chairman thus elected is entitled to retain the chair until the close of the proceedings; but should the statutory, or regular chairman, put in an appearance, it is usual for the temporary chairman at least to offer to vacate the chair.

This contingency, however, arises but rarely. Appointed chairmen usually may be trusted to arrive punctually. If they are not present when their meetings should begin, it is probably because of serious illness or other grave causes (of which the secretaries have been notified) which will keep them away altogether. The habit of punctuality is only what we have a right to expect from them. The despatch of business is made needlessly difficult by a late start.

Other Formulas Needed.—The procedure described in this chapter and in the special chapters each devoted to a closer examination of some special phase of it is, for the great majority of meetings, the best possible. There are, however, classes of meetings for which it is unfitted. Included in this category are assemblies called together to draw up the articles of new clubs or associations.

A concrete example will best enable us to make this unsuitability manifest. The employees of a business house, we will suppose, have been called together to inaugurate a contributory pension scheme. When the meeting opens many of those present have no clear idea of what is to be put forward. The proposed scheme is stated. When it is before the meeting for discussion an employee fastens upon some clause that will, he thinks, work inequitably. The sponsor of the proposal shows that the objection is based upon a misconception. Everyone is satisfied except the objector, who now misunderstands the explanation. A few minutes' give-and-take between him and the sponsor will see him completely satisfied. Can this be denied because the rule of regular debate is "One Man, One Speech?" Of course it can't, and because it can't the chairman often throws the reins on the shoulders of the meeting as if there existed no rules applicable to it. In this he is mistaken, there is a formula entirely suitable, that of the House of Commons in Committee. Under this everyone is allowed to speak without rising from his seat, to speak as often as he likes, and to have any motion he may propose put to the meeting, even if unseconded.

Debating Society Formula.—For debating societies (exclusive of local parliaments, which go through the forms of legislating, and follow, almost slavishly the procedure of the House of Commons) the accepted rules of public meetings are unsuitable for reasons precisely opposite to those we have just considered. Instead of the "One Man, One Speech" rule needing to be relaxed, it here needs to be drawn tighter and made "One Speech in the Course of the Evening." With perhaps two hours, all told, at the disposal of the members, it would be intolerable for one of their number to speak both upon motion and amendment or upon two amendments.

In another respect amendments can be a nuisance at debating societies. Usually their members are afraid to speak extemporarily. They arrive at the meeting with voluminous notes in their breast-pockets, and can be observed taking surreptitious glances through them while the proposer of the motion is speaking. What is a sympathetic chairman to do if all these intending speakers to the motion are anticipated by some old hand who proposes an amendment? If it is allowed, these precious "notes" are but spoilt sheets of paper, and a dozen prepared and rehearsed speeches must go undelivered. Our own solution of the difficulty would be to appeal to the old hand's good nature, and ask him to postpone his amendment until near the close. We wonder that debating societies do not provide in their rules for the postponement of amendments until the last hour, if not for their prohibition. There is very little need for them when the *sole* object is the practice of public speaking. This can be had quite well upon the motion announced.

Platform Propaganda.—It is not surprising that a set of rules intended to secure free and equal discussion between members whose rights are equal should be inapplicable to gatherings whose avowed object is the triumph of one side, and whose constituents are a few people who have been announced to speak and a larger number who have been invited to listen. Among the latter there prevails a hazy notion that they have all the rights, if they choose to insist on them, of a deliberative assembly, and the chairman, who in effect always suppresses any claim to exercise these imagined rights, has much the same belief, and when he forbids open debate is secretly afraid that he is robbing fellow Britons of their birthright of free speech. Let him be quite easy. If it is right to arrange platform propaganda, and who can doubt that it is, provided the object is worthy, the formula must be conducive to propaganda and not destructive of it. By this test the audience at a platform meeting has *not* the rights of a deliberative assembly or of a company meeting. If anyone in the body of the hall could rise at will and propose an amendment, a handful of malcontents by proposing successive amendments could prevent all but the first two of the announced speakers from obtaining a hearing. On these terms leading men could not be secured for the platform nor considerable audiences for the body of the hall. Oratorical propaganda would cease. Platform meetings, therefore, very properly have a formula of their own. The chairman's first care is that the object of the meeting should be achieved. Consistent with that he allows the meeting all the deliberative freedom possible. And that is all there is to it.

CHAPTER III

GENERAL MEETINGS OF COMPANIES.

THE custom of converting small businesses into Limited Companies, which often has many advantages, has become so prevalent that a business man with little previous experience of companies may find himself a director. Should he be offered the chairmanship, let him not be overawed by the responsibilities attaching to the position; for, as chairman, he will be able to protect his financial interests in the company. Presumably he is well acquainted with the operations of the concern (possibly it is his own business which has been converted into the company in question). True he lacks knowledge of Company Law; but although the subject is not altogether simple, he may acquire in these pages, supplemented by reference to a standard authority such as Sir Francis Beaufort Palmer's "Company Law" and to the Companies Act itself, sufficient knowledge for normal needs.

The Companies Act lays down the general law that applies to all companies, but it intentionally leaves many minor but not unimportant details to be provided for by the company's own regulations. These regulations are termed "The Articles of the Company." Nevertheless the Act provides a model set of Articles which apply to any company limited by shares that does not elect to draw up special Articles of its own. This model set of Articles is to be found in Table A of the First Schedule to the Companies Act, 1929, and is commonly referred to as Table A. Companies registered under the Companies Act of 1867, or under that of 1908 and which did not elect to have special articles of their own continue to be governed by the provisions of Table A of the Act under which they were registered.

In the following pages the provisions of Table A of the Companies Act, 1929, will be discussed, but it must always be remembered that Articles of a particular Company may differ from it.

Of Company General Meetings.—General Meetings, at which any shareholder in or any member of a club or company, or society is entitled to be present, are either Ordinary or Extraordinary; the former being those ordered annually to be held by the articles or rules of the society—which is really a statutory requirement. Meetings other than these, or arising out of them, are Extraordinary General Meetings or Special General Meetings, and may be convened by the directors or at the request of shareholders.

The proper notice having been given and the general or special business mentioned, the general meeting assembles at the hour fixed.

Chairman.—"The chairman, if any, of the board of directors shall preside as chairman at every general meeting of the company. If there be no such chairman, or if at any meeting he is not present within fifteen minutes after the time appointed for holding the meeting or is unwilling to act as chairman, the members present shall choose some one of their number to be chairman" (Articles 47 and 48, Table A).

Where a company has its own articles these often provide that in the absence from a general meeting of the chairman of directors, another director (if there are directors present and willing) shall take the chair. If this cannot be done, the members elect one of themselves to the chair.

The chairman of the board, let us say, then occupies the chair, in accordance with customary practice, and he will ascertain the number of shareholders present. If there is a quorum he will proceed.

Quorum of Members.—"No business shall be transacted at any general meeting unless a quorum of members is present at the time when the meeting proceeds to business; save as herein otherwise provided, three members personally present shall be a quorum" (Article 45, Table A).

"If within half an hour from the time appointed for the meeting a quorum is not present, the meeting, if convened upon the requisition of members, shall be dissolved; in any other case it shall stand adjourned to the same day in the next week, at the same time and place, and if at the adjourned meeting a quorum is not present within half an hour from the time appointed for the meeting the members present shall be a quorum" (Article 46, Table A).

(A half an hour being the limit of time allowed for the assembly of a quorum, it is idle to criticize, but in our opinion it is too long for ordinary people. Fifteen minutes' grace is quite enough for any man of business, and we think a half an hour is excessive. The punctual members are punished and unpunctual ones are encouraged, and even then no business may be practicable if the full quorum have not met.)

Whipping Up a Quorum.—If the number present does not reach the stipulated minimum no power on earth can avail in the transaction of business. The meeting is abortive. It is, however, open to the chairman, of his own initiative, to "whip-up" enough members or shareholders to constitute a quorum. He will not hesitate about this if important business is on hand.

Quorum of Members and Shares.—The object of the quorum rule is to ensure that business—which may be of first-rate importance—shall be done neither irregularly nor by too small a number of persons, who might, moreover, abuse their powers. In the case of shareholders, sometimes the number of shares held as well as the holders themselves, count in the direction of a quorum. So a specified number must, in this case, hold a certain amount of the share capital of the company before the quorum is made.

The great majority of companies have articles or rules that lay down the numbers and qualifications that constitute a quorum.

Preliminaries—Agenda.—It is an obvious convenience to circulate beforehand, generally in the document summoning the meeting, a memorandum of the topics to be discussed. On the day of the meeting, the secretary must take care to provide the chairman with a full agenda paper of the business, numbered in the order in which the subjects will be taken.

Formalities and Essentials.—The necessary quorum being present at the proper time, the chairman states the fact and proceeds to business. He will have the secretary of the company and in many cases the company solicitor beside him to assist in the settlement of any legal questions or in the statement of any matter of business that has demanded, or may demand, the opinion of the solicitor or of counsel. (Throughout the business the secretary never intervenes publicly, save at the call of the chairman, whom he must keep posted in all the necessary details. That is why he usually sits beside the chair.)

Minutes.—After his declaration that there is a quorum present, the chairman's first step is to call upon the secretary to read the notice of the meeting and then the minutes of the last meeting. This done, the chairman asks permission of the shareholders to sign the minutes. If no question is raised, the chairman signs, and the minutes thus signed and attested are legal evidence of proceedings. For this reason the people who had sanctioned the proceedings must be extremely careful to see that their words and directions are correctly recorded. In the event of legal proceedings, it may be necessary to put in the Minute Book as evidence, but the minutes of the last meeting may not have been signed. In this case the chairman can sign, for though it is customary to sign at the next succeeding meeting, he is not bound to wait.

If any question as to their faithful representation of the previous proceedings is raised at the general meeting, a discussion will be initiated by the chairman, but strictly and solely to the point at issue. In law, minutes once made *and signed* must never be altered by the deletion or addition of anything.

The Minutes and their Value.—The minutes embrace all proceedings and resolutions of the committee, board, or company, and their correct entry and neat transcription are absolutely necessary in face of the Act.

(For the form that the minutes should take see page 128.)

Report and Accounts.—The chairman will then proceed to business, and if the report and accounts of the company (and its directors) are to the fore, he will in his speech to the meeting refer to both, and in all probability analyse the accounts. The report having been already circulated, will be "taken as read" on the motion, duly seconded and carried, of someone in the meeting.

The chairman should subsequently move "That the report and accounts be adopted." The chairman is the right person to do this since if he is also (as is almost certain to be the case) chairman of the board, he will be more familiar than anyone else (save the general manager) with the details of the matters treated of in the report. Someone will rise and second this motion, and then the question of their adoption will be proposed to the meeting by the chairman. "The question before the meeting is that the report and accounts be adopted." (This is sometimes called "Stating the Question.")

Discussion by Members.—Now the time has arrived for the inevitable discussion; and as each shareholder, or member, rises in his place, the chairman must ascertain who he is, and announce him by name, so that those present—or the reporters, if any—may be aware of the speaker's identity.

Putting the Question.—When the discussion of the accounts etc., has come to an end—and the chairman will not bring it to an abrupt close—it will be his duty to reply to strictures and criticisms or to acknowledge gracefully congratulation and eulogies. He may have to do both. In concluding his remarks, the chairman will put the question—viz., "That the report and the accounts be adopted. Those who are in favour of the motion please hold up one hand. Those against!"

The Vote. The Poll.—The hands will be held up and counted and the chairman will declare the accounts passed or not, as the case may be. Someone might have demanded a poll, but fortunately no one has, thus enabling us to consider that difficult and thorny subject at length in our next chapter.

Table A has something to say about this vote by show of hands (Article 50). "At any general meeting a resolution put to the vote of the meeting shall be decided on a show of hands unless a poll is demanded . . . . Unless a poll is so demanded a declaration by the chairman that a resolution has on a show of hands, been carried, or carried unanimously, or by a particular majority, or lost, and an entry to that effect in the book of the proceedings of the company, shall be conclusive evidence of the fact, without proof of the number or proportion of the votes recorded in favour of, or against that resolution."

Article 52. "In the case of an equality of votes, whether on a show of hands or on a poll, the chairman shall be entitled to a second or casting vote."

Article 54. "On a show of hands every member present in person shall have one vote.

Article 57. "No member shall be entitled to vote at any general meeting unless all calls or other sums presently payable by him in respect of shares in the company have been paid."

These are the articles governing voting by show of hands in companies that do not possess their own articles.

Other Business.—The chairman then proceeds to the other business, such as the declaration of dividend, re-election of retiring, or election of new directors, and so on.

Let us suppose that the necessary business having been completed some one wishes to move a resolution, or to submit some proposal to the meeting.

Permissible Resolutions.—Without here going into the details of procedure as to motions and resolutions, which form the subject of Chapter VI, it may be as well to remark that every motion brought forward must have relation to the business of the meeting at the time. Any other should be ruled out of order, and no motions other than those for the furtherance and progress of the purposes of the meeting, should be permitted.

The duty of the chairman is herein clear, but by no means easy. "Many men many minds" is a motto which receives much exemplification in a meeting, and the chair may come to loggerheads with members upon the subject of the fitness of the motion for discussion. We have known cases in which the chair has been both appealed to, and remonstrated with, by other members against, and in favour of, a speaker who had in one instance been challenged by a member, and on another occasion checked by the chairman. There are meddlesome people at most meetings, but the chairman should not hesitate to keep them in order. Controversy with the chair is not only unseemly, but it is likely to be accepted as proof that the president is a weak man.

Amendments.—Unless at a special meeting, anyone can move an amendment, though sometimes amendments are purposely excluded by the terms of the notice of meeting. Such exclusion, however, seems of doubtful legality, since there is a *prima facie* right to propose a relevant amendment. The amendment must, of course, keep within the terms of the notice aforesaid. If not it cannot be put from the chair.

A discussion may arise upon this point of Order—whether the amendment be admissible. The company's legal adviser, who should be present upon these occasions, can decide such fine points, and the chairman will do well to be guided by him on all matters involving legal niceties.

Putting Amendments.—The amendment is put shortly at company meetings, thus:—

"The original question was, 'That so-and-so.'
"To this an amendment is moved, 'That such-and-such.'
"Those in favour of the amendment hold up one hand.
"Those against the amendment hold up one hand."
Then the verdict is pronounced, and business goes on.

In company meetings the procedure as to amendments is somewhat strictly interpreted. For instance, if, *inter alia*, the notice intimates a proposal to increase the capital by £30,000, an amendment to double this amount would be construed as irregular, since it would be held improper to call members together to consider a definite and limited proposal, and confront them suddenly with a much larger one. The assumption is good that absentee members stayed away because they had no objection to the proposal as set forth in the notice. Where, on the other hand, the proposal in the notice was couched in much more general terms, as, for instance, merely "To increase the capital," this will afford wide scope for amendment. The chairman must, therefore, examine the notice paper very scrupulously and see that there is no vital variation from it in the agenda or the terms of any amendment which may be handed in during the meeting. He must not refuse a relevant amendment, even if he be under the belief that it is *ultra vires*, since this refusal might invalidate the resolution which the amendment was drawn up to modify. Even if the mover of the amendment omits to challenge the chairman's decision there and then, this omission will not jeopardise his right to impeach the resolution. It is evident, therefore, that at company meetings the chairman, unless himself an expert, should, for self protection, insist upon the attendance of the company's legal adviser. A point that chairmen should keep in mind is that unless the regulations otherwise provide, an amendment need not be seconded if put and voted on (see page 62).

Withdrawal of Amendments.—An amendment may be withdrawn on the same terms as a motion (see page 58).

To the question of amendments generally and the form that they should take, a whole chapter is devoted (see pages 61–4).

Courtesy to Members.—A chairman is not compelled to give a member a hearing, and of course a meeting can "howl" anyone down if it does not wish to listen to him. But unless in peculiarly warlike circumstances, and in a heated atmosphere, such drastic measures are not often resorted to. "Bear and forbear" should be the motto of every meeting, and "speak gently" that of each member. Moreover, it is clearly the duty of the chairman to do his best to obtain a hearing for every person whom he has permitted to speak. If this person promises to be long-winded, a gentle hint from the chairman himself will generally suffice; while if he wander from the point or depart from order, it is the chairman's function to intervene. Prompt, firm, but courteous action on the part of the chairman will often avert turbulence in the meeting. For this reason, therefore, he should never relax his vigilance, but keep a close watch upon the course of events. He should never suffer the control of an assembly to pass out of his hands, owing to the presence of masterful, or, it may be, noisy members in the meeting.

Vote of Thanks to the Chair.—We have now sketched the course of an ordinary general business meeting of a company limited by shares, from the announcement of the presence of a quorum through the reading of its minutes, the discharge of its necessary business, and the desultory discussion that often concludes it. Nothing remains now but the customary *vote of thanks* to the chairman. This may be signed by the proposer in the minute book, but this act of courtesy, more often than not, is omitted.

Societies, clubs and charitable organizations may with advantage adopt the procedure of public companies, not following it slavishly where different conditions demand a different routine, but, on the other hand, not departing from it except for some very good reason.

Directors' Meetings.—Table A directs that:— (Article 81) "The directors may meet together for the despatch of business, adjourn, and otherwise regulate their meetings as they think fit. Questions arising at any meeting shall be decided by a majority of votes. In case of an equality of votes, the chairman shall have a second or casting vote. A director may, and the secretary on the requisition of a director shall, at any time summon a meeting of the directors."

(Article 82) "The quorum necessary for the transaction of the business of the directors may be fixed by the directors, and unless so fixed shall, when the number of directors exceeds three, be three, and when the number of directors does not exceed three, be two."

(Article 83) "The continuing directors may act notwithstanding any vacancy in their body, but if and so long as their number is reduced below the number fixed by or pursuant to the regulation of the company as the necessary quorum of directors, the continuing directors may act for the purpose of increasing the number of directors to that number, or of summoning a general meeting of the company, but for no other purpose."

(Article 84) "The directors may elect a chairman of their meetings and determine the period for which he is to hold office; but if no such chairman is elected, or if at any meeting the chairman is not present within five minutes after the time appointed for holding the same, the direc-

tors present may choose one of their number to be chairman
of the meeting."

These articles give the law as to election of chairman and
quorum at directors' meetings.

Companies Without Share Capital Limited by Guarantee.—
Compared with companies limited by shares these companies are comparatively few. Mutual insurance clubs are
companies of this nature. A member does not take shares
in order to get a dividend, but to obtain the advantages
of pooling his marine risks with those of other members.
The great majority of companies that register as companies limited by guarantee, are, however, associations
incorporated for the advancement of some public object.
The liability of the members of these concerns, whether
philanthropic or otherwise, is limited to such amount as
they may undertake to contribute to the assets of the company
in the event of its being wound up (Companies Act, 1929,
Section 1).

The articles of association of such a company are to be
found in Table C of the First Schedule of the Companies
Act, 1929.

(Article 11) Table C. "No business shall be transacted
at any general meeting, unless a quorum of members is
present at the time when the meeting proceeds to business;
save as herein otherwise provided, three members personally
present shall be a quorum."

(Article 12) "If within half an hour from the time
appointed for the meeting a quorum is not present, the
meeting, if convened upon the requisition of members,
shall be dissolved, in any other case it shall stand adjourned
to the same day in the next week at the same time and
place; and if at the adjourned meeting a quorum is not
present within half an hour from the time appointed for
the meeting, the members present shall be a quorum."

CHAPTER IV

POLLS AND PROXIES.

In our last chapter we ran through the procedure at a typical company meeting and found that it was very much the same as that obtaining at other meetings. We have now to consider contingencies that may arise to perplex an inexperienced chairman or even one of considerable experience if this has not included presidency of meetings of limited companies; for these are features peculiar to such gatherings. Of course, the chairman has the assistance of the secretary (whose efficiency may be assumed), but shareholders can be argumentative, and the chairman who cannot repel a questioning of his rulings without a whispered conference with the official beside him cuts but a poor figure.

No one wishes to be as futile as was George Nupkins, Esq., Justice of the Peace, addressing Mr. Pickwick, who had been brought before him. "I call upon you to—I think that's the course, Mr. Jinks?" "Certainly, sir." "To—to—what, Mr. Jinks?" said the magistrate pettishly. "To find bail, sir." "Yes. Therefore I call upon you—as I was about to say, when I was interrupted by my clerk—to find bail." Meetings are quick to detect it when a chairman's omniscience hangs upon such "interruptions." Fortunately there is not a great deal to be mastered, and the law on the subject is stated very clearly by our old friend Table A.

Demand of a Poll.—We may suppose a debate closed. All the speakers for and against the motion have had their say, and the question is put by the chairman in the usual manner:

"The question before the meeting is 'That so-and-so' [reading it]. Those who are of that opinion hold up one hand [counting them]. Those who are of contrary opinion hold up one hand [counting them]."

But a poll may be demanded. That is, someone in the audience is of opinion that the chairman has erred in his conclusion, or some large shareholder wishes the vote to be taken in a way that gives full weight to his holding and to the holdings of those who have sent him their proxies. This person, therefore, challenges the decision as soon as the chairman has announced it, and demands a poll.

When a Poll Shall be Granted.—To be effective this demand must come from at least three members, or by one or two members if he (or they) hold not less than 15 per cent. of the paid up capital, and be made before or on the declaration of the result by show of hands. Otherwise the vote by show of hands is decisive (Article 50, Table A.) Here as elsewhere in all that concerns meetings of companies limited by shares, the Act applies only when the company does not possess articles of its own. In this matter of poll the articles of a company are likely to be the same as those of the Act with certain qualifications. Person or persons (for in small companies sometimes a single member has the right to demand a poll) must have, let us say, a certain holding or share capital in the company; or certain conditions may be attached to the demand, such as the number of persons who shall demand it, or that it must be made in writing, a precaution which the person demanding usually observes by having the demand already written out in his pocket. Whatever the conditions the chairman must see that they are carried out.

The person or persons will demand the poll in writing, stating their names and holdings of shares, and the motion upon which the poll is demanded.

Their qualifications having been verified by the secretary, for which purpose the share register should be in evidence, the chairman will make the necessary announcement respecting the poll to the meeting.

Time and Conditions.—The chairman will then fix the time and the place for the poll, which may be taken immediately, or may be fixed for a future date if it is desirable to have the votes of all the members, or of some members not present at that meeting.

The poll, even if not taken there and then, is to be deemed as part of the proceedings at the meeting, for though another day is appointed for it, this is not an adjournment. It is, however, not uncommon to adjourn to hear the result. If not completed on the day on which it is begun, the poll must be continued subsequently, for the chairman may not close it so long as voters are coming in.

Five articles in Table A may be quoted:

"If a poll is duly demanded, it shall be taken in such manner as the chairman directs, and the result of the poll shall be deemed to be the resolution of the meeting at which the poll was demanded" (Article 51).

"In the case of an equality of votes, whether on a show of hands or on a poll, the chairman of the meeting at which the show of hands takes place or at which the poll is demanded shall be entitled to a second or casting vote." (Article 52).

"A poll demanded on the election of a chairman or on a question of adjournment shall be taken forthwith. A poll demanded on any other question shall be taken at such time as the chairman of the meeting directs." (Article 53).

"On a show of hands every member present in person shall have one vote. On a poll every member shall have one vote for each share of which he is the holder." (Article 54).

"No member shall be entitled to vote at any general meeting unless all calls or other sums presently payable by him in respect of shares of the company have been paid." (Article 57).

But, generally, the number of votes must depend upon the rules of the company, for Table A is not suited for every company, and nearly every private company possesses its own articles of association, and need not adopt Table A.

Postponement of Poll.—If the poll is not immediately taken, it may be very awkward, and so ordinarily the poll is proceeded with at once, and the iron is struck while hot. But, as a usual practice in important questions, the poll is taken on the next day, or the next but one, when members can vote if competent to do so.

Summary Poll.—As regards the directions as to taking the poll in such a manner as the chairman directs, it has been urged that if the poll, as in Table A, is to be taken in accordance with the chairman's instructions, it is doubtful whether it can legally be taken at once. Nevertheless, Lord Justice Buckley, one of the greatest authorities on the subject of company law, entertains no doubt on the matter.

"If, by the regulation the poll is to be taken 'in such manner as the chairman may direct', a poll may be taken there and then." (Chillington Iron Co., 29 Ch. Div. 29.)

This is the law of the matter.

The chairman must note that though not present when a poll was demanded, a member may nevertheless vote, and, further, that to shut out and exclude a voter may invalidate a poll.

Method of Polling.—When a poll is taken, members usually write their names for or against the motion on a list prepared for the occasion by the secretary. This list or form gives the information required respecting the voters, their number of shares, etc., whether by proxy, etc., and the votes, whether for or against the motion.

Anyone can then see at a glance the state of the poll, and whether the proper conditions have been complied with.

Scrutineers are usually appointed by the meeting or the chairman to examine and count the votes and report the result to the chairman. This precaution should never be omitted.

When the poll is "closed," the votes are counted and the report made to the chairman, who will announce the result to the meeting. This is a very simple matter, though in some instances the personal votes and the proxies are taken separately, and then added together.

Proxies.—Proxies are permissible under certain restrictions which the articles commonly lay down.

"On a poll votes may be given either personally or by proxy." (Article 58, Table A.)

The proxy paper is generally impressed with a (penny) stamp; sometimes the stamp is merely stuck on the instrument. The stamp in this form should be cancelled by the person executing the proxy, either by placing his initials and the date on it, or by otherwise marking it so as to render further use of it impossible. A proxy stamped thus is only available for one meeting or any adjournment of it. If meant for more than one meeting it must bear a ten-shilling stamp.

The form of instrument appointing a proxy is described in Article 61, Table A.

"The instrument appointing a proxy shall be in writing under the hand of the appointer or of his attorney duly authorised in writing, or, if the appointer is a corporation, either under seal, or under the hand of an officer or attorney duly authorised. A proxy need not be a member of the company." (Article 59. Table A.)

"The instrument appointing a proxy and the power of attorney or other authority, if any, under which it is signed . . . shall be deposited at the registered office of a company not less than forty-eight hours before the time for holding the meeting or adjourned meeting at which the person named in the instrument proposes to vote." (Article 60. Table A.)

"The instrument appointing a proxy shall be deemed to confer authority to demand or join in demanding a poll." (Article 62. Table A.)

Proxies, as such, are not available when voting is by holding up the hand, in the usual manner—a "show of hands" as it is termed. On these occasions members must vote personally.

Abstention from Voting.—Numerous instances have arisen in which some members, though present, have not recorded their votes. They have listened to the discussion, but have abstained from voting upon some plea, perhaps thinking that any responsibility is thereby avoided, or being unwilling to vote against a friend or to agree with an enemy. "Trimming" is not wholly without its penalties, however, since it may afterwards appear that the vote, on one side or the other, was of final importance.

In Parliamentary practice, we know, the member must vote if he is present in the House at the Division, and, equally, no member can vote unless he happens to be present when the Speaker puts the question. But, obviously, this procedure does not obtain outside the House. There is no compulsion in the matter in ordinary meetings.

"Trimming."—Nevertheless, we have known cases in which members, by declining to vote after hearing the discussion, have fancied that they neither countenanced nor disapproved of a measure—members who wished to please both parties, and who had no opinion of their own, apparently, upon the question.

Upon such a matter as this it would be foolish to dogmatise. If a shareholder who has heard both sides of a proposal, has been convinced by neither, he is within his rights to refrain from voting altogether. His vote is a right of property, which he may use as he thinks fit, his judgment being entirely unfettered. It is even possible for him, in some cases, to bind himself to vote, or not to vote, in a particular way. In the last resort he, surely, may be permitted to manage his own affairs in his own way. He will suffer in the event of a mistaken decision.

CHAPTER V

CHAIRMAN AND MEMBERS.

Chairman's Duty to Members.—No chairman should resent inquiries—such as are customary at company meetings—as personally offensive or detrimental to his dignity. He should answer questions simply and explain any point (in the Report, we will say) that has been misunderstood or not understood, or have this done under his authority by the company secretary or solicitor. Even if the disgruntled shareholder prove slow to see that his fancied grievance has been explained away, the chairman should not show impatience, but be tolerant of honest stupidity, resisting temptations to score off it. The Johnsonian "Sir, I have supplied you with arguments, but it is not my province to furnish you with the brains to understand them" is a perfect example of how *not* to address a troublesome shareholder.

The chairman should bear in mind that the interrogator's only fault is slowness of understanding. Apart from this his refusal to accept explanations that don't satisfy him is plucky and wise. Nothing is so dangerous in business as to pretend to understand what one does not. Often the man "who wants to know, you know" is a very small holder, and sometimes, we are sorry to say the chair has less patience with him on this account. This is inexcusable.

A shareholder who has entrusted his money to the care of a certain body of men has a legitimate right to inquire concerning the use those men are making of it. To attempt to browbeat him because his holding is comparatively small is cowardly and mean. The shareholder may have invested all he had, and to find fault and be captious, because he seeks information regarding his whole available capital, is not only wicked and contemptible, but in itself almost justifies some amount of suspicion of the company's standing and prospects. A chairman of this description is rarely encountered, and in many meetings would not be tolerated.

At the same time a chairman has his rights as well as his duties, and if confronted with sheer rudeness and insolence will be expected to uphold the dignity and authority of his position, and to maintain his self-respect.

Power of the Chairman.—The chairman of a meeting is rightly invested with very great power and influence, and on that account should be most careful not to lower his office by unseemly conduct. A strong chairman will be strongly supported, because he knows his own mind; and he may rest assured that numerous shareholders who do not know their minds upon a given matter, will follow his lead like so many sheep. 'Tis excellent to have a giant's strength, but tyrannous to use it like a giant.

Arbitrary Conduct of Chairman.—Nearly always the heat of a discussion is the result of friction between the directors and shareholders. The friction sometimes reaches such a height that a stormy scene ensues, in which personalities and undignified accusations are exchanged.

"Order !"—The chairman, supported by his directors, will, of course, exert himself to keep order. Usually it will suffice to call "Order! Order!"; but if there is any official conspiracy to stifle discussion because the company's record is not clean and clear, the meeting will not, and should not, allow itself to be browbeaten by the chair, which is likely to be most arbitrary when the previous mismanagement has been most flagrant.

There is, however, no warrant for this kind of conduct, and shareholders should not allow themselves to be bluffed out of their rights. They will accomplish more by resolute and concerted action at the meeting, and by fully exercising the power that their votes give them than by appeals to the Courts, which are very loth to interfere in the internal economy of registered companies, arguing very rightly that shareholders should be strong enough to act for themselves. As they elected the chairman, let them now depose him. They have the power; let them wield it, and not go crying to their legal protector to save them from their quondam friend.

The Specious Chairman.—The chairman, if unscrupulous, becomes even more dangerous when his iniquities are hidden by speciousness and charm of manner. Such a man may hoodwink the shareholders and ruin them, a result to which his high position in society, his apparently unblemished character, his suavity and open-handedness, all and each contribute.

Shareholders who seriously distrust the management should insist that either their doubts be removed or the causes of them, and must not allow themselves either to be cajoled, or to be bullied into uneasy acquiescence. Eternal vigilance is the price of solvency.

Member's Duty.—It will now be perfectly plain that every person present at a meeting is, to a certain extent, answerable and responsible for what passes. He countenances the proceedings by his presence, and, therefore, may be held to be a consenting party; even his absence may not wholly purge him of responsibility for untoward events, for, having had notice of the purpose for which the meeting was called, he cannot plead ignorance of the nature of the business to be done. Having had the opportunity to attend, and being acquainted with the business on the notice-paper, he might have been able, by protest and speech, to frustrate any tactics of a doubtful character. Had a prior engagement, or the state of his health prevented his personal attendance, he could, in most cases, have been represented by proxy, or have sent a temperate but reasoned letter with a request that it should be read to the meeting. This request would no doubt be ignored, if everything were not open and above board, but even so, the privilege of a letter to the editor of an influential journal is at his command.

It is therefore a duty, if sometimes an unwelcome duty, to attend the meetings, and to hear the proceedings. No doubt, we can read the report in the newspapers, or in the printed statement of the proceedings, but this may be more exasperating than helpful, especially if it appears that questions were asked and answered in which we were keenly interested, and on which, had we been present, we could have enlightened the meeting.

The Manners of Members.—It is not only the chairman who needs a reminder of the desirability of urbanity and fair play: shareholders have also a duty in this respect. It is incumbent upon everyone to assist in keeping order in the meeting, to preserve silence when silence is desirable, but to insist upon the meeting being treated fairly, and each member impartially.

On the whole, members do behave themselves. The presumption is that they are present to facilitate business and, all being above board, are prepared to co-operate towards that end. Something, however, is often lacking in their tolerance of the unwanted speaker. It is, doubtless, galling to have one's time wasted by incompetent or verbose speakers, but nothing will be gained by yielding to the temptation to "guy" the unfortunate orators, probably unconscious of the sorry figure they are cutting.

Quenching a Bore.—The easiest and most dignified manner of quenching the "bore," or the too fluent speaker, or the obnoxious one who is present in nearly every meeting, is to rise and move that the question be now put to the meeting.

If the motion is seconded and carried, the obnoxious one is quenched. If not, the minority must grin and bear it, or leave without voting if they are in a hurry, since, as the votes have proved, a majority holds that the person in question is not a bore—or at least not on that occasion at that moment.

Where a meeting has confidence in its chairman it can safely wait for him to convey a hint to one of his henchmen when patience has been stretched sufficiently.

So far we have been considering the behaviour of shareholders at company general meetings. It will be convenient here to extend the subject to members and audiences generally.

Unfit Members.—In local council and similar meetings feelings sometimes get the better of those present; and can any spectacle be more ridiculous and more condemnatory of the unfitness of the rulers to rule when they cannot even govern their own tongues? In the halls where local authorities hold their meetings, one often feels disposed to recommend that the motto "Better is he that ruleth his speech than he that taketh a city," should be boldly displayed.

A Good Sign.—Of course, we are not referring to difference of opinion in any meeting, but to the undesirable manner in which controversy is too frequently conducted. A sheep-like docility is always to be deprecated. It is a healthy sign when members rise and contend in honest and considered argument, without personal rancour or anger. But the duty of everyone to his neighbour should be observed, and while sentiments may be held up to ridicule, the expounder of them should be exempt from abuse. To show respect for a speaker and contempt for his opinions is a combination hard to achieve (impossible unless the derision be accompanied by some friendly recognition of the goodness of the motive behind them) but impersonality of reference is a help. "The gentleman who suggested so and so" may in effect be the same as "Mr. Richards," but that gentleman when referred to thus does not feel so acutely that he is being pilloried. Similarly, in the hope of giving an impersonal aspect to discussion we have the House of Commons practice (except in Committee) of describing speakers as the "Honourable Member for this or that constituency," instead of alluding to them by name. To carry on discussion with the most sparing use of personal names undoubtedly keeps it on a higher plane.

Obedience.—Again, each member should, as a matter of order, support the chairman. Everyone should remember that the "chair" is the ruler, and that each one is bound to sustain him. No member should dispute the chairman's authority or ruling. By all means let him use every effort to prevent the choice of the same man (if his incompetence is unquestionable) a second time, but for the moment the chairman is supreme, and his office must be respected.

To the Point.—The speaker for or against a motion should remember that the time of a meeting is valuable. He should not travel away from the subject he is attempting to elucidate. Let him be clear, well-informed, concise. Let him never insinuate anything against an opponent. Such a line of advocacy brings its own condemnation. The insinuation, like the stab in the back, is deadly; and though it may be denied and refuted, the wound and the effect may remain.

Untrained, heedless, or thoughtless speakers often mar the effect of what might otherwise be a good speech, by the imputation of motive. If they feel bound to denounce a policy or an argument, let them do so with all the earnestness of their nature, but no good purpose will be served by charging their opponent with unworthy motives. It is only the man who has no case, and knows it, who abuses the opposing attorney.

The Golden Rule.—The man who speaks only when he has something to say that is worth saying is always safe to command an appreciative hearing. The audience has almost an instinct for the man who knows his subject and can marshal his facts. To such it is ever a pleasure to listen, and frequently fullness of knowledge and an artless display of it will compensate for the want of rhetoric and eloquence.

CHAPTER VI

MOTIONS AND WITHDRAWALS OF MOTIONS.

IT will be useful to consider in some detail the nature and scope of motions generally, including in our survey not only motions moved at company meetings but also those at meetings of every kind where discussion is open.

Notice of a Motion.—Notice is customarily given of motions with the precise terms in which they are to be submitted to discussion. By the necessity of the case no notice can be given of the "Previous Question," nor, as a rule, of a matter of privilege or contempt, which may have emerged, so to speak, "all of a sudden."

Right to Move a Motion.—Every member has a right as a member to make a motion, or to second one, and to speak upon it, if he is in order. However unwelcome he may be as a speaker, or however generally unpopular his known views may be to the majority, the chairman must assist him in putting his resolution. If it is not seconded, it drops, so indignant members may calm themselves by the reflection that if there is no other support the infliction will soon be over. A minority, even a minority of one, has rights, and a high-handed denial of them, whether by chair or meeting, may have serious legal consequences.

Motion must be Relevant.—The motion is, or ought to be, in accord with the aims of the meeting as set forth in the notice of advertisement calling it. Of this the chairman will assure himself. His ruling upon the subject is final.

A Motion must Affirm.—When the mover rises, he should read from a slip of paper his proposition, which he should be careful to frame in the affirmative. A motion must

always affirm, never deny. Something is, or something is
to be! "That so-and-so shall," or "is to be," is the framework of the motion. To this rule, that every valid motion
shall affirm, there is no exception apart from the "Previous
Question" resolution when put in accordance with the present
House of Commons formula, and even here we think the
affirmative is preferable. (See page 56.)

A Motion must be Seconded.—The mover having read the
proposition, it must be seconded. This is imperative, but,
as already explained, may be done very briefly—either by
raising the hat, as in the Commons, or in a brief speech, or
by simply rising and addressing the chair with "I beg to
second that proposition." If the seconder does not speak,
he may exercise his right at a later period of the debate.

The chairman, having seen that the motion has been
seconded, reads the motion, or requests the secretary to
read it, so that its tenor may be grasped by all. This in the
House of Commons is called "proposing the question." In
other assemblies, it is often called "stating the question."
We consider this preferable. By the uninitiated, "proposing
the question" is apt to be confused with "putting the question
or motion," *i.e.* putting to the vote.

Putting a Motion.—If no seconder is found, the motion
lapses at once. But if no one rises to discuss it after it has
been moved and seconded, the chairman will put it to the
meeting. He must be careful to put the question both "for,"
and "against," for he must not infer, from the fact that the
motion excited no discussion, that therefore it would not be
opposed. The opinion of the meeting will be taken by a
show of hands, and the majority, of course, decides the
question.

If there is no opposition, "carried *nem. con.*" is a safer
formula for the chairman to use then in announcing the
meeting's decision than "carried unanimously." All may not
have concurred, although none has contradicted.

Motions put "en bloc" and "seriatim."—The occasion
was a general meeting, and the motion was that the Committee
of the institution be re-elected—as previously—*en bloc*.
This motion was seconded, and the chairman rose to put the

question, when an amendment was made that each member of the committee be elected separately.

This amendment was seconded, and the new question put to the meeting. It was carried, and so seven different motions had to be made, seconded, and put to the meeting, every one of the questions being carried without any dissentient voice, although the alteration in procedure had been carried by a large majority of the meeting.

Of course the incident just alluded to was comparatively trifling, but it might happen that a motion upon a subject includes several clauses, and if so, an amendment might be carried requiring the motion to be put clause by clause, each clause as a separate motion.

In this way a long debate might be initiated and carried on, because anyone could speak upon each new question, as put from the chair, though as a matter of practice the general and, in truth, the real debate takes place upon the first clause of the motion, as speakers to that usually say all they have to say upon the whole subject, and practically whittle the debate down to the discussion upon the first paragraph before them.

Nevertheless, the various clauses must be proposed and put, whatever the chances of the speakers may be in the end regarding the later clauses. This is perhaps an extreme illustration, because greater care is ordinarily shown in the drafting of motions.

The " Previous Question."—The "Previous Question," which is often moved, is merely a device for avoiding the decision on the motion proposed without stifling or burking discussion of it. The subject may be of interest and importance, expressions of opinion may be harmless and even valuable, and yet a vote either of "yes" or "no" to the motion now might embarrass the executive. The "Previous Question" rescues them from this dilemma. The embarrassing vote is not taken, the right of free speech is not curtailed, and if the "Previous Question" has been moved, as it should be, not from the chair but from the meeting, supporters of the motion do not feel that there has been any discrimination against them on the part of the management. Of course the mover of the "Previous Question" *may* have had a quiet hint from the chair.

Procedure on the "Previous Question."—A motion has been made, let us assume, and seconded in the usual way. The question has been "stated" by the chair, and debate upon it is in progress (or, perhaps, about to begin) when some member who feels that a vote upon it is undesirable rises and says, "Mr. Chairman, I move the 'Previous Question'." He may then, if he likes, discuss the original motion, as may the speakers who follow him, the moving of the "Previous Question" not having affected the course of the discussion, except as regards the right to move amendments. It is the vote not the free discussion that is attacked. No amendment can be made to a motion after the motion for the "Previous Question" has been made. No one may move the "Previous Question" who has spoken upon the motion, or has moved or seconded an amendment to it, nor may it be moved when an amendment is before the meeting. But when the amendment has been settled, and the original or "amended original" motion is again before the meeting for the final vote, the "Previous Question" may be moved. The mover of the "Previous Question" has not the right of reply. When the time comes to put the motion for the "Previous Question" to the vote, the chairman uses this formula. (Another form which we think inferior is described later):—"That the original motion be now put." The proposer of the "Previous Question" and his supporters vote against the resolution. (This is the one and only contingency in which a proposer votes against the motion that he has originated.) If the motion "That the original motion be now put" is carried, the original question again holds the field. But it cannot be further discussed. It must be put to the vote immediately. If the motion "That the original motion be now put" be rejected, the "original question" disappears automatically, and the meeting passes on to the next business. A point arises here as to the possibility of a member reintroducing the original motion at the next sitting; for remember, it has not been actually rejected. Analogy says "No"; the decision of the members that a vote on this motion is inadvisable is entitled to as much respect as any other decision. But as there is no universal rule about this, every society or corporation should make a rule—that the original motion cannot be re-introduced in whatever time period is most convenient. The "Previous Question" can be moved in committee.

Alternative Formula for "Previous Question" Motion.—
Sir Reginald Palgrave holds that the formula (as given in our
previous paragraph) "That the original motion be now put,"
which until the other day was employed in the House of
Commons, is inferior to a still older Parliamentary usage
recorded in the Journals of the House—"That the original
question be *not* now put"; and his suggestions have been
adopted at Westminster. The main advantages he claims
for the negative form is that it removes the necessity that
supporters of the "Previous Question" were under of voting
against their own resolution. To his formula "That the
question be *not* now put" the mover of the "Previous Question" of course votes "Aye." Admittedly, this is an advantage, so far as it goes. Against this is the great disadvantage
that the phrase "Be *not* now put" breaks the rule to which
(apart from this) there is no exception whatever, that every
valid motion shall affirm. With all respect to Sir Reginald
we hold that the affirmative formula "Be now put" is the
better, and in this we have the support of the vast majority
of those who have a practical knowledge of the subject.

The rule as to "Previous Question" as explained by Sir
Reginald Palgrave is as follows:

"A motion for the 'Previous Question' (*i.e.*, 'That the
question be not now put') shall for all purposes of order
be dealt with as an amendment. It shall take precedence
over all other amendments." And again:

"The proposal for the 'Previous Question' is prefaced
with the words used in proposing an amendment, thus:
the chairman says:

"'The original question was this; that, so and so, etc.,
Since which the "Previous Question" has been proposed.
The question is: that the original question be not now put'."

"That Question" and "This Question."—People who have
only a slight experience of public meetings and deliberative
assemblies are sometimes puzzled when the word "that"
is substituted for the words "the original question" in the
motion put from the chair. The meaning is the same; the
"Previous Question", as the most recent is "*this* question,"
the original has become "*that* question." Nothing is gained
by the use of this somewhat pedantic formula. "The original
question" is self-explanatory.

Motion for Adjournment.—The motion for adjournment has been mentioned, and should be commented on. This motion may be made at any time during a debate, and may be repeated, with some little necessary variations, frequently. It is another method of setting aside an undesirable motion, or of obstructing business, but should not be indulged in by anyone not sustained by the majority, for it is an invidious motion, save when used for the perfectly legitimate purpose of postponing a debate until a more convenient season.

As soon as ever the motion for adjournment of the meeting, or "That the Chairman do leave the Chair," is moved and seconded, the chairman is compelled to put it immediately in the usual form—thus:

"The question is that this meeting be adjourned"; or, "The question is that the chairman do now leave the chair."

If this is carried, the meeting stands adjourned; but sometimes an amendment is moved to fix the time or date of resumption of proceedings. Then the question is again put in the usual formal manner.

Movement of Adjournment Rules.—But the motion for adjournment cannot be made or supported by any person who has already intervened in the debate upon the specific motion then before the meeting, nor by anyone who has moved or seconded an amendment to that motion. The same rules apply to motions for adjournment as to the "Previous Question," and until a new question is put, no one who has already spoken in connection with the "present" motion, can be permitted to intervene.

Of course, the very fact that someone has made a motion for the adjournment, and that it has been seconded, releases the former speakers. The embargo is immediately removed, because a new question has been put from the chair, and the original motion sinks out of sight temporarily.

We have, then, considered the manner and the procedure of making a motion. The motion is declared in a sentence, affirmatively, crystallised and preferably short, but it may be split up into several motions, each of which had to be proposed separately, seconded, and put to the meeting.

Withdrawal of Motions.—Not infrequently it happens that the mover of a resolution has been completely satisfied, and, it may be, answered by the turn the debate has taken, and sees no reason why he should press the matter at issue to a division. Now and again it may be deemed necessary to teach a busybody a lesson and give him a thorough drubbing by voting his resolution down by a huge majority. Speaking generally, however, the desire to retreat from an untenable position, or from a line of counsel, conduct, or criticism which has ceased to count is commendable, and no obstacles are interposed. But a certain course of procedure must be followed. The mover has no power to withdraw, since a motion when moved and seconded has passed beyond his control, and, belongs to the domain of the meeting. Nor has the chairman any right of interference. The mover is at the mercy of the meeting. Having intimated to the chairman that he has no wish to go to a vote, and having obtained his seconder's consent, the mover asks permission of the meeting to withdraw his proposition. The chairman thereupon proposes: "That the motion proposed by Mr. —— be and is hereby withdrawn by leave of the meeting." If carried, this will convey the desired freedom to the mover and seconder, and any minutes that may be taken of the incident will merely record that the motion was "withdrawn by leave."

Mover must Act.—As described, the method of withdrawal is very simple and, without impropriety, the chairman may facilitate it; but the procedure must originate with the mover. It is a mistake to suppose that his seconder has the right to take the first step, although his consent to withdraw must be obtained and recorded, as was made clear in the previous paragraph. Of course, if the mover is obliged to leave the meeting, he may, by courtesy, intimate his desire, and allow the seconder to continue the negotiation. But the latter can never be the prime mover.

This withdrawal must be arranged and carried out before the original question is submitted to the vote. The mover may be satisfied in the manner already mentioned, or may perceive that his motion has no chance of success, and even that the vote will cast some amount of obloquy or ridicule upon the sponsors.

Why the seconder cannot act may not be evident at once. But a little reflection will make it clear. It is curious but true that at public meetings some men are prone to yield to sentiment. Thus they often second a proposal, not because they take any particular interest in the subject of it, but because they "feel for" the mover in his solitary position—as it were, "one against the world"—and so they weakly second his motion just to enable it to be discussed. As long as there exists suspicion about the seconder's *bona fides*, so long will he not be suffered to lead.

Withdrawal of a Motion to which an Amendment has been Moved.—But what happens if an amendment has been proposed to a motion which the mover wishes to withdraw? To withdraw an original motion to which an amendment has been moved, the chairman must ask the meeting to agree to the withdrawal of the amendment.

Such amendment, if made, cannot be withdrawn, even with the consent of the meeting, unless the mover and seconder (or certainly the mover) of the amendment agree to this course.

The chairman, therefore, upon the expressed desire of the mover of the original motion to withdraw his proposition after the amendment has been made—but not put to the meeting—must obtain the sanction of the audience, with the consent of the mover of the amendment, that it may be withdrawn.

There are thus wheels within wheels; the mover of the amendment must assist in getting his proposition out of the way before the original motion can be backed out.

If the Amendment is Negatived.—Should the amendment have been put, and negatived, the way is clear, and the mover of the original motion may proceed to withdraw it by leave, as explained.

If Carried.—If, on the other hand, the amendment has been put and carried, of course the original motion is no more and, being non-existent, cannot be withdrawn. In such case, however, it is difficult to imagine its mover asking for permission to withdraw it. He must act earlier.

The chairman should clearly dissociate the arguments concerning the motion for withdrawal from the main question, and permit only the former subject to be discussed (when once it has appeared) until it is settled.

CHAPTER VII

AMENDMENTS.

Object of an Amendment. The amendment usually substitutes another form of words for the original motion, and is generally framed with this intention. A direct negative to a motion, as cannot be too often repeated, is not a legitimate amendment. Such a refusal, or rejection, is effected by voting against the motion. The amendment modifies, trims, or suggests an alternative to the original motion. Thus someone may move as an amendment, to insert certain words after "That" with which the motion begins. Numerous instances occur in the course of parliamentary debate, of amendments "to leave out certain words " of the original motion, which thus may become an entirely fresh proposition. The amendment must clearly intimate whether its object is to amend or banish the original motion.

Notice of Amendment.—We have seen in the last chapter that it is customary to give notice of motions, with the precise terms in which they are to be submitted to discussion. The case is different with amendments. There is no reason why it should be so in those instances in which the exact form of a motion is made known, it may be several days beforehand, and one does occasionally find that notice of amendment to such and such a motion is announced in advance. There is great convenience to all concerned in the practice, which should therefore be encouraged as far as possible. But when the terms of a motion are not stated until the moment of its introduction, it is clearly impracticable for the mover of an amendment, however much he may wish to consult the general convenience, to intimate before-hand the character of his amendment.

61

Amendments resemble motions in that they must be relevant, must affirm, and may be proposed by any member. As regards the need of seconding there is a difference.

Seconding Amendments.—Although, by almost universal usage amendments are refused by the chair if they fail to find a seconder, the necessity of a seconder is not recognised by law. This was settled by the ruling of Sir Francis Beaufort in the Harbury Bridge Case. "Unless the regulations otherwise provide, an amendment at a meeting need not be seconded if it is put and voted upon." But, of course, where the articles of a company require a seconder, no unseconded amendment can be proceeded with. Generally a company or institution has its own rules. But where it hasn't the chairman should beware of refusing to put an unseconded amendment to the vote if the proposer insists upon the opinion of the meeting being taken.

The seconder of an amendment must make his speech, and advance his argument at the time he rises to second the amendment. He cannot by a merely formal seconding reserve his right to speak later in the debate as can the seconder of a motion. He has no right in the discussion that follows his seconding to interpolate any remarks, as arguments. It is, however, permissible for him to speak again when that amendment has been disposed of. For instance: When a new question is raised by an amendment, or by a new motion, and such is proposed by the chairman, it is competent for any member to rise and (if permitted) to speak upon the amendment or the motion newly put. This liberty does not extend to an adjourned debate upon the same question, though it applies to the motion for adjournment which raises a new question.

"Proposing" or "Stating" an Amendment.—An amendment is usually brought forward by the chairman, after he has read the resolution—in the following manner:

"Gentlemen,—The original question was this, 'That the salary of the Architect of our Board be increased by an annual sum of fifty pounds,' since which an amendment has been proposed to leave out the word 'fifty' and substitute 'one hundred.' This has been seconded, and the subject is now open for discussion, unless you prefer to proceed at once to the vote."

Amendments—When Put to the Vote?—It is scarcely too much to say that except in Parliament, the custom of submitting an amendment to the vote before the motion which it seeks to amend is practically universal. The method is extremely simple and, in public meetings especially, simplicity should be aimed at. Every step in reaching a decision is clear. The amendment is put first and is either carried or lost. If carried, the original motion vanishes, and the amendment itself becomes the substantive motion, *and must be put again as such*. It is now competent to propose another amendment to it (which must, of course, be relevant), and if this is carried it, in turn, will become the original motion, and so the debate may go on until, by a process of exhaustion, the final opinion of the meeting has been ascertained. But if the first amendment is lost, the original motion is still before the meeting, and before putting it to the vote the chairman will ask whether any other amendment is forthcoming, and if not will put the motion itself to the meeting.

Sir Reginald Palgrave condemns the universal custom under the impression that the merits of the original motion are lost sight of when it and an amendment are both under discussion at the same time. He cannot see that supporters of either or both are entitled to lay their views before the audience with such force of argument as they can command. Before the vote is taken all that can be reasonably urged in favour of either proposal has been urged, and if the audience declare for the amendment by an absolute majority on the count of the show of hands, why should a motion which has been thus rejected be still regarded as possessed of vitality? It has been killed by vote, and is rightly looked upon as extinct.

Amendments to Amendments.—Occasionally an amendment is moved upon an amendment. In this event the amendment No. 1 is put forward into the position of an original motion— or substantive motion—itself. The true original motion retires out of ken for a while, and the amendment it gave rise to steps into its place. This is a cumbersome and confusing method of eliciting opinion and, though not unknown in Parliamentary practice, is decidedly inferior to the more usual and more popular manner of approach, whereby after one amendment has been disposed of another may be proposed. Procedure is simplified, and the audience more readily grasps the issue. A chairman should always prefer the customary to the pedantic or academic style.

Forms of Amendment.—The amendment may take different shapes. It may be what it purports to be, merely an amending or supplemental form of the motion, modifying either the language or the scope thereof, or it may be more or less contradictory to its principle or objects. So much is familiar to all who attend meetings. But the wording of them, the terms in which they are put, are not so familiar, and we have known listeners become hopelessly bewildered by the various amendments. Such persons often ended by voting for the views against which they had been roundly inveighing a few minutes before. The forms of amendment are given in detail in Chapter IX, "Parliamentary Procedure." A careful reading of these will elucidate the whole matter (which really isn't very difficult) and save the reader from the absurd mistakes to which we have just referred.

CHAPTER VIII

CLOSURE.

The Necessity.—There is a great tendency to speak inherent in some men. The majority are too diffident to rush in, but if irrelevant matter is permitted or speeches of inordinate length are not checked, business will certainly suffer. It often occurs that a meeting is needlessly prolonged by some person or persons, and sometimes this is done of set purpose to reduce the meeting to impotence. Greatly as we may dislike any limitation of the right of free speech, there must be some formula for dealing with obstructionists and extreme bores.

The Danger.—The dangers are apparent. The formula may be abused and employed to suppress not irrelevant speech, but unpopular speech (the telling of unwelcome truths, for instance) to silence not the malicious obstructionists but the too faithful friend. It is particularly the province of the chairman to see that this necessary weapon is not used tyrannically. However unpopular a speaker or his principles may be, the chairman must listen courteously and see that the meeting does the same. In a broad sense the chairman is the guardian of minorities, and must use due diligence to procure fair play. But majorities also have rights, and there are times when it is absolutely necessary for the conduct of business to resort to the Closure—the weapon of majorities.

The Closure.—Any detailed discussion of the forms of closure is of necessity academic, because most assemblies and every public meeting have long had an effective method of bringing debate to a permanent or temporary close, without inflicting much hardship upon anybody.

Closing a Debate Gently.—If the mind of the meeting is evidently made up, practice sanctions the closure being proposed by means of a motion, "That the question be now put." Anyone may rise and make this motion which, if seconded, must be put to the meeting by the chairman, who will allow no debate and who must not be intimidated or interrupted in this obvious duty, although at the meetings of some public bodies, as distinguished from public meetings, he has a power of veto.

If this familiar form of closure is carried, the amendment or motion under discussion must be put to the vote forthwith.

Putting the Closure.—The motion thus made to put the question will necessarily cause an interruption of the person who is then speaking, unless, as is the better and more considerate course (if there is room for courtesy in the circumstances), the motion is made at the close of a speech. But such an interposition is quite within the mover's rights while a member is speaking, and the motion may be made, according to the practice of some meetings, after the debate has been continued for an hour. As to such a proceeding, however, it is very arbitrary, and the chairman must take care not to countenance any high-handed action. It was, no doubt, to avoid anything of the kind that a right of veto was vested in the chair.

If the Closure is Carried.—If the motion for the putting of the question is carried by those present, the member who made the original motion under dispute should be called upon to close the debate in reply (ere the closure is acted upon); but he will be wise to do so quickly and cut his remarks as short as possible.

Right of Chairman to Quench Speech.—It is within the province of the chairman to warn a member, or speaker, to discontinue his speech if he persists in useless repetition and is evidently engaged in a policy of obstruction. And the chairman may, in certain circumstances, call someone else to proceed with the discussion, and failing him, require the original mover of the question to reply to the discussion, and then close the debate by putting the question in the usual manner.

"Next Business."—Motions for proceeding "to next business," or for the adjournment, as well as for the closure, may also be made, but in all three cases, common sense, and common practice, decree that no speeches be made by the seconders of such motions, while the mover of the first two may not exceed five minutes, and had better be content with a formal proposing. The closure, we have already said, must be put without debate.

Failure of Closure.—Should the motion be decided in favour of the continuance of the debate, and the motion for the closure be rejected, a reasonable period must elapse before another motion for adjournment or closure is permitted.

This second motion must be regulated in the same manner as the foregoing, and should not be made and seconded by the same persons who moved and seconded the former question for adjournment or closure. The reason for the latter proviso introduces us to the interesting but unwritten law of the courtesies of debate. It is with a view to avoiding the appearance of persecution that these two motions should not be moved and seconded a second time by the same persons at the same meeting.

The Chairman's Duty—The Chairman must, in all circumstances, be firm and decided in his procedure, careful to be within the rules and regulations governing the company or board; and in any legal point he should seek the assistance of the solicitor, who should be present. In the absence of the legal adviser, the chairman should consult the acts, articles, and notice of the meeting, which govern all the proceedings of the meetings of members of Joint Stock Companies. It is hardly necessary to add that order must be strictly observed, and no interruption permitted—points with which we have dealt in an earlier chapter.

Closure in the Commons.—In our next chapter on Parliamentary Procedure, will be found on page 72 the rule for putting the question which governs the House of Commons.

CHAPTER IX

PARLIAMENTARY PROCEDURE.

We will now briefly direct attention to certain details of Parliamentary Procedure that throw light upon the subjects discussed in Chapters VI and VII on Motions and Amendments.

Notices of Motion.—As most folk are aware, the Orders of the Day in Parliament constitute the Agenda of the House. The Notices of Motion are given by members named by the Speaker in succession from the list before him. When a member is thus called upon, he rises, reads his Notice, and seats himself as soon as convenient. This procedure is repeated until the list is exhausted.

It often happens that the member when called upon does not wish to give the intended Notice, generally because he perceives that the chances of his being heard on that particular day for which he has put down his name are small, in consequence of others being before him.

He, therefore, courteously raises his hat, and bowing to Mr. Speaker, who has called him, thereby intimates that he does not wish to accept the place on the list which has been allotted him.

This position on the list before the Speaker is a matter of chance, for, though each member desirous of giving Notice has written his name on the list—numbered in the margin, and ruled—the calling early or late is a matter of lot.

Suppose a ruled paper with numbers in the lefthand margin. Against each number (say 1 to 40) a member writes his name. There are then duplicate numbers put into a ballot-box, and when business begins the clerk at the table, like Jack Horner, "puts in his thumb" and pulls out a number—whichever he happens to seize. It may be No. 1 or 40, or any inter-mediate number.

The clerk then announces the number. The Speaker looks down the list for, say, No. 24, as announced, and calls out the name of the member which is written opposite 24 on the paper. He thus gets first choice of the days vacant within a month,—unless Government has appropriated all the time of the House!

Putting the Question.—In the House of Commons the division is first taken upon the original motion, and not on an amendment, save in Committee of Supply, when the popular method is followed and the amendment is put first. Suppose a bill is introduced: the original motion is "That the Matchbox Bill be now read a second time," and someone has moved an amendment "That the word 'now' be omitted and 'this day six months' inserted." The Speaker then states the facts as follows—mentioning the title of the bill—in the prescribed form, viz.:—

"The original motion was that this bill be now read a second time.

"Since then, an amendment has been made to leave out the word 'now' and insert the words 'this day six months'." These words, as all the world knows, are the recognised forms in which the *coup de grâce* is administered to many bills.

Voting.—On the original question the House will divide, and as the division goes so is the Speaker's decision. Those members in favour of the proposition "That the bill be now read a second time" (the original motion) will say "Aye!" those in favour of the amendment will say "No!"

The Speaker then declares his impression of the sounds, and whichever side he imagines has the more voices he declares "has it." "I think the 'Ayes' have it," he may say. But the "Noes" deny this, and the House is closed for a division, two tellers being appointed on each side—those on the Government side being the whips, the mover and seconder being tellers for the amendment they made.

Division in the House.—Two minutes by the glass is the period allowed for members to come in, and many are at times shut out. The reading-, writing-, and dining-rooms, the smoking-room, and the terrace are deserted when the electric bells ring and the hour-glass is running faster than the members themselves. Then the cry of "Order!" announces that the sand is run out. The doors are locked, and no one can enter now. Silence in the House!

The question is put to the House—full again—and then the "Ayes" and "Noes" file off into their respective lobbies right and left, the "tellers" in pairs one of each together. The clerks "tick" off the list of the men as they file in. The tellers count the members as they pass into either lobby, and, after the division, state the numbers to a clerk at the table. By and by the result is handed to the Speaker, who announces it to the House.

Should the numbers "tie" the Speaker gives the casting vote. The motion is thus carried or negatived, and the bill is ordered to be read a second time or it is withdrawn.

Tellers.—No division can be taken unless there are two "tellers." If only a single member challenge the decision of the Speaker as to the "Ayes" having it, he will be required to name his tellers should he persist in his defiance of the expressed wish of the House.

The Speaker of the House, or the Chairman of Ways and Means, may, in gauging the sense of the House, determine the limit of discussion, and "put the question" if a motion be made to that effect on his suggestion.

The Speaker or Chairman may also stop an irrelevant speech.

Those who desire to read up the subject will find an exhaustive account in the work on "Parliamentary Practice," by Lord Farnborough, who is probably better known to the majority of folk as Sir Thomas Erskine May.

Amendments.—The forms of amendments in Parliament are those which omit words of the motion, those which insert words into the original motion, and those which act both ways—viz., leave out some words and insert others.

Students of Parliamentary Procedure will remember the formulæ employed:—

"That the words proposed to be left out stand part of the question."

"It is suggested or proposed to insert so-and-so," etc.

"That the words 'so-and-so' be omitted, and the words 'such-and-such' be inserted instead thereof."

Amendment by Omission of Words.—Let us take for purpose of illustration a suppositious motion:—"That the salary of the Medical Officer be increased by a sum of £50 from this date, on approval by the Committee."

An amendment is moved to this to omit the words "on approval by the Committee." The amendment being seconded, the chairman rises and says.—

"The question was that the salary of the Medical Officer be increased by a sum of £50 from this date, on approval by the Committee.

"An amendment has been proposed to leave out the words 'on approval,' etc.

"The question I have to propose is, That the words 'on approval by the Committee' stand part of the question."

The amendment is then open to general discussion.

Votes.—When the amendment has been sufficiently discussed, or after it has become clear that no one beside the opener and seconder wishes to speak upon it, the members present will vote, and their votes, for and against, are counted. In the case of an equal number upon each side, the chairman will give a casting vote.

In this case, if the "Ayes" have it, the amendment is, of course, lost. The words remain, and the motion is open for discussion in its original form.

If, however, the "Noes" have it, the amendment is made, the words, "on approval by the Committee" are omitted, and the chairman puts to the meeting the motion. Thus:—

"The question as amended [or the main question as amended] is 'That the salary of the Medical Officer be increased by £50 from this date '."

The voting is then proceeded with, and the officer receives the addition to his salary.

Amendment by Inserting Words.—A different formula is adopted when the amendment seeks to insert certain words into the original motion.

Supposing that to the motion an amendment was proposed to insert the words "of the Shillinghill Institution" after the words "Medical Officer," the chairman would proceed in the way already indicated, by stating the original question; then he would say:—

"An amendment has been proposed to insert the words 'of the Shillinghill Institution' after 'officer.' The question is that the words suggested be inserted."

The amendment, if carried, to that extent alters the original motion, which is put as amended.

But if the amendment is not carried, the motion is put to the meeting in the original form.

Amendment by Substitution of Words.—Precisely similar procedure to that adopted when the amendment takes the form of omission of words is followed upon the occasion of the substitution of words in lieu of others.

Closure in the Commons.—It may be of service if we quote in full the rule for "Putting the Question" which governs the House of Commons:—

"When it shall appear to Mr. Speaker or to the Chairman of Ways and Means in a Committee of the whole House during any debate, that the subject has been adequately discussed, and that it is the evident sense of the House or of the Committee that the question be now put, he may so inform the House or the Committee; and if a motion be made 'That the question be now put,' Mr. Speaker or the Chairman shall put such question, and if the same be decided in the affirmative, the question under discussion shall be put forthwith.

"Provided that the question 'That the question be now put' shall not be decided in the affirmative, if a division be taken, if, in the opinion of the Speaker or the Chairman of Ways and Means, the motion is an abuse of the rules of the House, or an infringement of the rights of the minority."

But there is this important proviso, which we may state in the words of the editor of Lord Farnborough's standard work, that if "when a division is taken, it appears by the numbers declared from the chair, that not less than a hundred members voted in the majority in support of the motion, it is decided in the affirmative."

CHAPTER X

THE CHAIRMAN OF A COMMITTEE.

WE do not propose to go into the question of the Chairman of the House of Commons Committee, or Chairman of Committee of the House, who assumes the place of The Speaker, and rules the debate or discussion. Nor, on the other hand, is it necessary to interest ourselves in the ordinary business of the club committee or such assembly, already treated of in the foregoing pages under "Meetings."

General Committees.—We propose, with the assistance of the directions laid down by Mr. C. Eales and Sir Reginald Palgrave, to devote a few pages to the proceedings of a committee appointed for some specific purpose by the House of Commons, or other representative body, and to glance at the approved rules which govern such appointments.

The Chairman.—As regards the appointment of chairman, we may properly follow the regulations sanctioned by the usage of the House of Commons in the case of Select Committees.

Special Committees.—It frequently happens that an investigation by men of varied and extensive knowledge is required. Therefore a special committee of an institution, or of the body of members of a society, is demanded. This assembly will contain men of expert knowledge, capable of weighing evidence, and of framing a report with clerical assistance.

Selection of the Members.—The requisite steps are accordingly taken to select the proper men, and this is done either by direct nomination or by selection confirmed at the meeting. The names are submitted to the general body of the members, who approve or disapprove, as they think desirable, until the committee is empanelled.

(As regards committees of directors, or of other committees, see later in this chapter.)

Quorum of the Committee.—The committee having been selected, the first question is to fix the number necessary for a quorum. This question of the quorum in Company meetings has already been considered (p. 32). Here one-third of the number of the committee may safely be accepted as the needed quorum. We find that of a special committee of fifteen, five is the number established by custom of the House of Commons, and in no case should less than three, or four, be the quorum when the committee numbers more than eight members. Two constitute an unsatisfactory quorum, and might open the door to collusion.

But the real objection to a quorum of two is that, in case of an insuperable difference of opinion, business will be brought to a standstill.

Minimum and Maximum.—Three, therefore, is the least, and twenty the greatest, number of a quorum of a committee ranging between ten and eighty members; one-third being the maximum general standard.

The quorum decided (and, in the case of Select Committees or General Committees of the House of Commons, Parliament fixes the number), the committee first sets itself to select and elect its chairman.

Order of Reference.—But there is usually what is termed an "Order of Reference," which lays down the lines upon which the committee's train is to run, and the limits of its conduct. Such an order can, of course, be either permissive or obligatory—that is to say, it can indicate or command the principles upon which the committee shall proceed. The body, or committee, appointing the Select Committee, can thus limit the functions of its creature, or it may give it wide discretion by ordaining that the committee "be empowered to do" such-and-such things. The loophole thus caused tends to widen the prospect of the business, while the decision that "the committee shall" do so-and-so closes up the ground and limits the powers of the members.

["Parliamentary practice ordains that notice should be given both of this instruction and of the Order of Reference. The nomination of a committee, and the names offered in amendment, or substitution, for those on the list also demand a notice."—*Palgrave.*]

Powers of the Committee.—The committee, thus furnished with powers and having its quorum fixed, is ready to elect a chairman. This is done at the first time of assembling.

Chairman of the Committee.—In the case of a Select Committee of the House of Commons, the Parliamentary routine, as in the election of The Speaker, is followed, viz., the "question" is put after a motion has been made, or it may be after various members have been nominated.

The secretary, or clerk, will then put the question—or it may be put by a temporary chairman, who occupies the position for the purpose, not being himself a candidate.

Procedure in Electing the Chairman.—If there are two or more candidates nominated, the question is put thus:—

"A motion has been made by Mr. ——, and seconded, that Mr. A. J—— do take the Chair of this Committee.

"Another motion has been made by Mr. ——, and seconded, that Mr. J. A—— do take the Chair of the Committee."

On this occasion the secretary or clerk puts the question: the first motion first. The question is—

"That Mr. A. J—— do take the Chair of this Committee." The members then vote in the usual manner, and if the "Ayes" carry the election, Mr. A. J—— ascends to the Chair. If the "Noes" have it, then the second motion is put and (possibly) carried. A third candidate may be proposed if Mr. J. A—— (candidate No. 2) is rejected. Generally, however, an agreed chairman receives the unanimous support of the members. The body being tolerably small, the qualifications of the various members are well known and the most suitable usually emerges by consent.

No Chairman.—In smaller committees a chairman may not be elected at all, or if elected may be prevented from attending upon some occasion. At such times a temporary chairman is nominated in his place. The chairman of such a meeting possesses all the rights and privileges of the appointed chairman and decides questions, when necessary, by his casting vote

Procedure of Members.—"In Committee" the member is not restricted in speaking, or to motions, as in Parliamentary Debate. He need not rise to address the Chair, as is usual in other Meetings; he can speak as frequently as he has a mind to; and he is not in need of a seconder if he wishes to "move." Thus it will be perceived that members of committee are not so confined in their procedure as members in a general meeting.

Again, a committee may adjourn itself at any time, or arrange to meet at any time the majority of members may decide. The decisions are arrived at by voting in the usual manner—and when arrived at should show no difference of opinion.

Members' Opinions.—It is contrary to practice and not admissible for any member to affix a contrary opinion to a report. (We remember an Army Select Committee showed such a deviation from rules; and Commissions are not governed by such a rule—witness the famous Minority Report of the Poor Law Commission.) "But no counter-statement nor protest from the minority should accompany any report."

"If a chairman signs a report it should only be by way of authentication."—*Palgrave.*

Committee's Report.—The report of the committee is generally drafted first, and considered, paragraph by paragraph, is subject to amendments as in ordinary cases, and the vote of the members is taken upon the question being put—"That paragraph (No. so-and-so)," or "paragraph (so-and-so) as now amended, stand part of the question."

The original draft is usually entered in the Minute Book, and is then considered to have been "read a first time." When this is accepted, the motion "That the draft report be now read a second time" is made—and is carried, let us say. It is then read as stated by paragraphs, which are successively passed as read or as amended.

[It may be that some other member may move another report. If so, when the motion is made to read the former draft report "a second time," an amendment is moved in favour of Report No. 2, and voted on as usual. It is necessary that both drafts shall be entered on the Minutes under their respective authors' names.]

"If any fresh paragraph be inserted or proposed to be inserted as the report proceeds, each paragraph is proposed as an amendment to the draft report."—*Palgrave*.

The report, when finished, is voted to be sent up to the House, or other body which appointed the committee, in the usual way, the question being put by the chairman of the committee "That the report," etc.

Fate of the Report of the Committee.—The report of the committee, whether in draft form or as a series of resolutions, is then sent in to the governing body, who are assembled to consider it—it may be, in general meeting—and it is proceeded with in the usual way, being read by the secretary to the meeting.

The chairman then may move that the report be agreed to, and it may be accepted at once.   But strict Parliamentary Procedure decides that the chairman shall move "That the report be read a second time," immediately.

This opens the door for criticism, as the first motion would do, and after the chairman's motion in any case members can disapprove, amend, and criticise the report of the committee, care being taken by the chairman that nothing contrary to the scope and object of the committee's report (and of the original instructions) is permitted to be raised.   Only relevant amendments can be considered, and these will, of course, tend either to the upsetting of the report, or to its reconsideration by the same or another committee.

But if the motion of the chairman as to the adoption (or second reading) is carried by the meeting, of course the question is determined, and no further discussion is permissible beyond word-amendments.   The meeting has, by its vote, sanctioned the principle of the report, and it cannot be rejected *qua* report.   It may, however, be polished up, so to speak, and in some respects modified, but the actual aim and object of the report cannot be altered—the body of it remains.

Submitting a Report for Consideration.—The writer has been on committees where such a course was adopted by the chairman on a draft report, which he read to the members. The report had been adopted, but was submitted for improvement, and discussed for effect, paragraph by paragraph,

several verbal amendments being made before the report
was finally agreed to.

When this climax had been reached, the meeting set about
the consideration of the means to be adopted for carrying
out the recommendations of the report. Suggestions were
made, considered, and decided on when, but not until, the
meeting was satisfied. This is the usual procedure. Attendance is usually pretty regular, and there is usually a sufficient
quorum at the appointed hour of meeting.

It may be remarked that in Parliament while The Speaker
is addressed by his title, the Chairman of Committees is,
when in the Chair, addressed by his name.

PARLIAMENTARY COMMITTEES.

Committee of the House.—If a measure has passed the
second reading, the House considers it "in Committee,"
which is, to all intents and purposes, the same as considering
it in the House—the Committee being "of the whole House,"
with a difference. The President is a chairman in a chair
set for the purpose, and members may speak as often as they
choose.

Subsequently the bill is "reported" to the House. This
is not a useless formality, for though the Committee is of
the whole House, in all probability comparatively few members
attend the Committee. This answers to the report stage
already mentioned, and the reported bill may be then amended
and even rejected. But if accepted by the Commons it must
pass the Lords ere it becomes law, subject to the provisions
of the Parliament Act.

Committee of Supply.—"Committee of Supply" needs no
explanation. Its meaning is evident.

Procedure in standing committees is the same as in select
committees. The quorum is twenty, the number of members
is between sixty and eighty, with certain provisos. The
chairman is selected from a certain "panel" of six, or not
less than four.

Standing Committees.—The reports of standing committees
are treated as reports of the "whole House Committee,"
provided that the provisions of the standing orders shall not
apply to bills reported by standing committees.

OTHER COMMITTEES.

Sub-Committees.—When the board of a company meets, it often happens that the members form various committees. A county council divides itself into finance, fire brigade, and numerous other committees, with a view to undertaking certain duties and reporting to the main body the result of the researches. The council then, by the general body of its members, decides upon the course to be pursued.

Such committees relieve the council, or the board which appoints them, of a considerable quantity of routine business and investigation or inquiry, which is not agreeable to everyone, but is of interest to some. To probe and investigate is to them a congenial occupation. So there are members who discharge these inquisitorial functions admirably for the board, or council, and leave the latter free to occupy itself with weighty and important matters, and with the consideration of the reports of the committees.

Rules for Sub-Committees.—Articles of Association or regulations sometimes provide that even one director may constitute a committee in himself. More generally the committee consists of three, or perhaps two members, and such committee is appointed by resolution of the board of directors.

A committee may likewise appoint some of their number a sub-committee to ascertain certain points connected with objects they have in view, and give the sub-committee power to deal with the question fully and even to carry out their decisions for the benefit of the society. But in all important business matters a report should be made, and the committee itself, or the board should decide the matters investigated, or submit them to the general meeting, according to circumstances and regulations.

Table A on Committees.—Table A (Article 85) provides that "The directors may delegate any of their powers to committees consisting of such member or members of their body as they think fit; any committee so formed shall, in the exercise of the powers so delegated, conform to any regulations that may be imposed on it by the directors."

(Article 86) "A committee may elect a chairman of its meetings; if no such chairman is elected, or if at any meeting the chairman is not present within five minutes after the time appointed for holding the same, the members present may choose one of their number to be chairman of the meeting.

(Article 87) "A committee may meet and adjourn as it thinks proper. Questions arising at any meeting shall be determined by a majority of votes of the members present, and in case of an equality of votes the chairman shall have a second or casting vote.

(Article 88) "All acts done by any meeting of the directors or of a committee of directors, or by any person acting as a director, shall, notwithstanding that it be afterwards discovered that there was some defect in the appointment of any such director or person acting as aforesaid, or that they or any of them were disqualified, be as valid as if every such person had been duly appointed and was qualified to be a director."

These clauses sum up the legal aspect of directors' committees.

CHAPTER XI

CHAIRMAN OF THE LONDON COUNTY COUNCIL.

So much interest is taken nowadays in local self-government and so many readers may wish or be invited to bear a share in it—a legitimate and laudable desire—that a recapitulation of the routine adopted by the London County Council, in so far as it relates to the functions of the chairman, will prove useful. There is this advantage in choosing, by way of illustration, the practice of one of the foremost governing bodies, that it may be easily modified to suit the wants of a smaller council. Where · necessary the summary is eluci-dated by comment, which will be found within brackets:—

Election.—No business shall precede that of the election of chairman.

(The reason for this is obvious.)

Term of Office.—The chairman's term shall be one year, but he shall remain in office until his successor has accepted office and subscribed the usual declaration.

(He himself may be re-elected.)

Quorum.—One-fourth of the total membership of the council shall constitute a quorum. If no quorum be present at the expiry of fifteen minutes after the hour at which any meeting of the council is appointed to be held, no council meeting shall be held. If, during any meeting, a member call the chairman's attention to the fact that a quorum is not present, he shall count heads and, if it appear that a quorum is not present, the meeting shall stand adjourned.

(The quorum rule prevents business being rushed through in a "hole and corner" fashion. The short fifteen minutes' grace makes for punctuality.)

In the Chair.—The chairman shall preside at all meetings at which he is present. In his absence the vice-chairman shall preside, and in the absence of both the deputy-chairman shall preside. Should all three be absent, then the members present shall elect one of their number to the chair.

(The absence of chairman, vice-chairman and deputy is a very remote contingency, but it must be provided for.)

Disorder in the Public Gallery.—If one or more persons is guilty of disorder in the public gallery, the chairman shall take the necessary steps for the ejection of the offenders and for their exclusion for as long a period as expedient.

Temporary Adjournment.—At the conclusion of any speech, the chairman may accept a motion for the adjournment of the meeting for a period not exceeding two hours, but no debate shall be held on such motion, which may provide that the proposal shall take effect at a specified time not later than one hour after the motion has been made.

Adjournment by Chairman.—In the interests of order the chairman is empowered to adjourn or suspend a session for a time to be named by him.

Special Meetings.—The chairman may call a meeting at any time, and shall do so upon receiving a requisition signed by twenty members. If he decline to summon it, the petitioners may thereupon summon it themselves. If he appear to consent but fail to call it within seven days of the requisition, the signatories may then summon such meeting.

Limits of Business.—With the exception of matters of urgency brought up in accordance with the council's standing orders, the business of a meeting shall be confined to the items mentioned in the summons calling it.

Order of Business.—For the due discharge of its functions the business shall be taken in the following order:—(1) Minutes of previous meeting; (2) Petitions; (3) Opening of tenders; (4) Report as to documents sealed since last meeting; (5) Questions; (6) Reports of committees; (7) Notices of motion.

Advance of Business.—At his discretion the chairman may bring forward any business at any stage.

Urgency.—Matters arising too late to be specified on the summons calling the meeting may be brought forward by the chairman, with the consent of a majority of the whole council, or of three-fourths of the members present.

(Every chairman is fallible, and it is therefore incumbent upon members to see that this action is wisely taken.)

Notices of Motion.—Notices of motion shall be in writing, and be entered in the Notice Book by the clerk in the order in which they are received, but every notice must be relevant to some question affecting the administration or condition of London. If need be, the chairman shall decide whether or not a motion is in order.

Demeanour of Members.—Members shall be uncovered while the council sits, when speaking, shall stand, and shall address the chair.

Chairman First.—Should the chairman rise during debate the member then in possession of the House shall resume his seat, and the council be silent, so that the chairman may be heard respectfully and without interruption.

(The idea underlying this order is the upholding always of the authority and dignity of the chair.)

Length of Speeches.—At ordinary meetings and during ordinary business, no member shall speak for more than fifteen minutes, save by consent of the council, which should be given only when the question under discussion is of exceptional importance. The council may extend the period by ten minutes. In very exceptional circumstances, as when the yearly budget is presented, still further latitude may be allowed, but always by leave of the council.

Irrelevance.—The chairman shall call any member to order for irrelevance, repetition, unbecoming language, or other breach of order, and may direct such member to discontinue his speech.

(These powers have been bestowed upon the occupant of the chair, partly to preserve the decencies of debate and partly to minimise obstructive tactics by mere talk.)

Disorder.—When there is grave disorder or persistent defiance of the chairman, he can direct the offender to retire, either for the remainder of the sitting or for some shorter period. If the offender will not retire, the chairman shall give direction for his removal and any other directions he may consider necessary for restoring order.

Order of Debate.—The chairman shall not permit any member to speak more than once to any motion or amendment. Only the proposer of an original motion has a right of reply which, the chairman must see to it, shall be confined to answering previous speakers and shall not introduce fresh matter of discussion.

(Obviously, it would be unfair to suffer the mover to strengthen his case by importing into his reply new particulars which members who have already spoken, and who cannot speak again had no opportunity of considering and, it may be, rebutting.)

As soon as the speech in reply is ended, the vote must be taken.

Procedure in committee is governed by much freer rules. Members may address the committee more than once on the same proposition and, greater latitude in procedure generally is sanctioned.

Points of Order.—But it is not a contravention of the regulation just mentioned to allow a member who has already spoken to rise to a point of order, or tender a personal explanation called for by the nature or course of the debate. The chairman shall decide whether the point of order or personal explanation be admissible, and his ruling shall be final and undebatable. Neither the point of order nor personal explanation can be subject of a fresh debate, nor shall either be supported by a speech. The point must be taken clearly and crisply, and the explanation must be strictly limited to the facts of the case.

Withdrawal of Motion.—With the consent of the council a motion or amendment may be withdrawn, but no debate on the point must take place. It is usual for the mover of a motion or amendment desirous of withdrawing to obtain the sanction of his seconder to this course.

Amendments.—The chairman shall take care that every amendment accepted by him—which must be in writing, and signed by the mover—is relevant. The mover may nominate his seconder, but no amendment can be discussed until it has been seconded. No member can speak more than once to an amendment, and the mover thereof has no right of reply. No other amendment shall be moved until the first one has been disposed of. If an amendment is carried, it (or the motion so amended) shall become the substantive motion to which a further amendment may be moved. No member can move or second more than one amendment to any motion.

(Though many speakers fail to realise it, the negative to a motion is not an amendment, the proper course in such event being always to vote with the "Noes" against the motion.)

Postponement.—At the end of any speech a member may propose the postponement of the consideration of the question for a stated period, or *sine die*, but he may not speak for more than five minutes, and his motion shall be seconded without speech. The mover of the question under debate shall have a right of reply for five minutes, without prejudice to his ultimate right of reply on the whole debate. The motion shall then be put *instanter*. If the postponement is carried to a fixed date, the question shall have precedence on the list of motions for such date.

Adjournment of Council.—At the close of any speech or any business, a member may propose the adjournment of the council, but he shall not speak for more than five minutes, and his seconder shall only formally second the motion. No debate shall be allowed, save that to the mover of the question under debate shall be granted five minutes for reply. The chairman may ask those who support the motion to rise in their places, and if fewer than ten other members stand, the motion shall not be proceeded with. If the adjournment is carried, the matter under debate shall be adjourned until the next meeting, unless dealt with at the stage of unopposed business, which may be taken before the council adjourn. No member may move or second more than one motion for adjournment of the council at the same sitting.

Adjournment of Debate.—The debate may be adjourned subject to similar conditions to those obtaining in respect of postponement of a question and adjournment of the council. If carried, the discussion shall be resumed at the next meeting, and the council shall proceed at its then sitting to the next business, the proposition being for the adjournment of the matter under debate and not for the adjournment of the council.

"That the Question be Now Put."—At the close of any speech a member may move—without debate, however—"that the question be now put," and, if this is seconded, the motion shall be put forthwith, unless the chairman rule otherwise. Should this be carried, the motion or amendment under discussion must be put to the vote at once. Similarly, any member may propose "That the chairman do proceed to the next business," and if this is seconded and carried, he shall immediately proceed to the next business accordingly.

Motion to Rescind.—No motion to rescind a resolution passed within the preceding six months shall be entertained, unless the notice be signed by twenty other members and be specified in the summons calling the meeting. Nor, when disposed of, shall it be competent for any member to bring forward a like resolution for another six months. This order does not apply to motions which are moved by the chairman or other members of a committee.

Assistance.—The chairman, whether of the council or of a committee, is entitled to look to the clerk of the council as his principal adviser, and for all necessary information and assistance in the conduct and despatch of business.

Quorum for Other Public Bodies.—The law regulates the number that shall form a quorum for borough, district, and county councils and the like; the number varying from one-fourth to one-third, save for special purposes, when it may be as high as two-thirds. It is obviously impossible to lay down a hard-and-fast rule, but the necessity for a quorum of considerable size on the part of public authorities is self-evident. In such a precaution lies the only safeguard against neglect of the public interest.

CHAPTER XII

"PLATFORM" AND "LIVELY" MEETING.

"Forewarned, Forearmed."—Save at times when political feeling runs high, or some purely local question has stirred up rancour and strife in a district, most meetings pass off quietly enough.

As we have considered pretty fully the duties and powers of chairmen at the meetings of deliberative assemblies, public companies, and the like, showing, amongst other things how a firm and judicious chairman can keep the meeting in hand, we propose in this chapter to limit the scope of our remarks to what may be called "Platform Meetings," gatherings that have been assembled, not for discussion, but for propaganda; not to debate, but to listen to what some famous orator (backed by one or two lesser celebrities) has to say in support of the views and objects of the society that has arranged the meeting. It is in meetings of this character that disorder has most often to be encountered.

Some men dislike a tame meeting; but there is an essential difference between a "live" and a "lively" gathering. The former goes off well at all points because of the prevailing harmony; the latter leaves an unpleasant impression because everything seems to have been "at sixes and sevens." Occasionally actual disturbance breaks out, and then the chairman's lot is not a happy one. In such circumstances, however, he must hold fast and sit tight. He is the captain on the bridge and must stick to his post until absolutely satisfied that evil passions have obtained the predominance and that a deliberate attempt at wrecking the meeting is afoot. Then, all his efforts to maintain order and keep peace having failed, he shall collect his papers and declare the meeting at an end. Timidity in such a crisis is a fatal policy, as it only tends to precipitate disorder which a firm and resolute attitude might avert. And the chairman of a "lively" meeting is not without guidance, which we now proceed to discuss.

Precautionary Arrangements.—As one never can tell what novelty may, in the legitimate course of business, be sprung upon a meeting—and it is the unexpected, we are told, that happens—the promoters should always take obvious precautions against possible malignants. For a meeting needs to be managed as systematically as any other enterprise, and the chairman is entitled to assume that the preparations have been properly superintended. Take the case of what is called an "open" meeting, that is, one to which admission is free. It may, nevertheless, be prudent to reserve a few of the front rows on the floor of the hall, a charge being made for them or the tickets being distributed judiciously, according to circumstances. When the cost of holding the meeting has been considerable, these reserved-seat tickets are often issued at a stated price to defray part of the expense. But money is not always an object. The presence of many supporters of the cause which the meeting is being held to advocate can only be guaranteed by reserving seats for them. Moreover, it is a great help to the chairman and "platform" generally, to say nothing of the reporters sitting immediately below the rostrum, to have, so to speak, a friendly body-guard right in front. Few things are better calculated to put a chairman out than to have an ill-mannered man just below him, interpolating rude remarks in a raucous voice. Still, the number of tickets at an ostensibly open meeting must not be overdone, as members of the audience, quite peacefully disposed, are likely to resent their being denied seats in good positions at a so-called free assembly. For meetings where the attendance is pretty sure to be large and the demeanour of the audience all that could be desired, it will yet be for the general convenience if a staff of stewards is enrolled beforehand to show people to their seats, to see that the seats are filled and no space wasted, to distribute (and sell, if need be) programmes, and to supply information, it may be, about the objects of the meeting, or the society which has called it. But such arrangements may govern every description of gathering, and precautions more adapted to prevent, not due opposition, but rowdyism, are needful.

Tickets.—We have seen that a certain number of tickets may be issued for reserved seats at meetings where no hostility is expected. But occasion may arise when admission by ticket is indispensable. It is very seldom that an engineered disturbance can be "kept dark." Some hint of it is sure to leak out sooner or later, and then the promoters must deal strongly with the situation that confronts them. One safeguard may be adopted which, although not a perfect specific, will go far to embarrass the enemy. No person is admitted except by ticket, on the face of which is printed a pledge that the holder of it will not disturb the proceedings and will accept the chairman's decision. A malcontent who might otherwise create a disturbance will refrain when his very presence is proof that he has used a ticket thereby giving a pledge not to disturb. But, of course, such a consideration will offer no obstacle to a hired and unscrupulous opposition. Then, again, it is possible to forge tickets. One can recall gatherings nullified by a wholesale forgery of tickets, the holders of which came to the meeting determined, by hook or by crook, to spoil it. It is rare that such deep feeling is provoked by any question of the day. Pledge-tickets may therefore be resorted to with reasonable hope of success in the vast majority of cases. Untransferable tickets for smaller meetings can be made a sufficient preventative of rowdyism by two precautions: their endorsement with the name of the person to whom sent, and their signature by the secretary, which makes a forgery of them criminal. This double precaution ensures that the actual user will be a respectable and responsible person. The only drawback is the extra labour entailed upon the secretary of writing perhaps five hundred names and making his own signature as often, in addition to that of despatching the tickets by post.

The Chairman's Powers.—Even when disturbance is anticipated, however, the personality of the chairman counts for much. A man of discretion, tact, good temper, and presence of mind may, by the judicious and not too masterful exercise of his personal qualities, accomplish more in the way of repressing unruly members, than by a strict insistence on his technical and legal rights. Just as a referee at football sometimes does more harm than good by "seeing too much," so a chairman may defeat his own ends and play the other side's game, by taking notice of every interruption. While, on the one hand, he must not expose himself to a charge of cowardice, on the other hand he must not be too eager to restrict the just freedom of his hearers. He must be prepared to cope with disorder or clamour when it really emerges, but it is never wise of him to betray that he believes or knows that disturbance is coming. Perhaps by his urbanity and fair dealing he may avert the threatened demonstration. On the appearance of antagonism, he should boldly intimate that he will take care to give opponents every opportunity, within reason, of asking questions, when the speech in course of delivery is finished. (Some famous orators, Lloyd George, for example, welcome interruptions, and score their greatest triumphs in impromptu retorts. Such masters of dialectics will pounce on interruptions regardless of anything the chairman may rule about a deferred consideration of them. So the chairman will not do any practical harm if he assume that all speakers need to be protected and can only do themselves justice when allowed to pursue the thread of their argument continuously.) An audience likes fair dealing, and hostile folk have speedily responded to the appeal *ad hominem*. Having given his word, however, the chairman must keep it. The bulk of the audience will heartily support the chairman, if he has conducted his strategy so far with scrupulous fairness but undoubted ability. In fact, generalship is a factor of supreme importance to the chairman of a "lively" meeting.

But the considerations which we have hitherto discussed do not exhaust the powers behind the chairman in his endeavour to assert his authority and maintain order.

Some Points of Law.—If the promoters of a meeting are wise, they will strengthen the position both of the chairman and of themselves, by giving due thought to certain preliminary matters; for the promoters possess some indubitable legal rights. As renters of the hall, or room, for the purposes of the meeting, they and they alone have the exclusive use of it for the time being, whether this be forenoon, afternoon, or evening. All who attend it, therefore, are there on sufferance; they are licensees whose license may be withdrawn at any moment. This furnishes the chairman with a powerful weapon. Supposing he espies the ringleader of the forces of disorder (and he may fortify his belief by reference to his nearest neighbour on the platform: there will be no harm in obtaining evidence of the fact), he publicly bids the offender leave the premises. His order is ignored both now and when it is repeated immediately afterwards. His next step becomes definite. The culprit has elected to defy the temporary tenant of the hall, whose representative or deputy the chairman is. Accordingly he is a trespasser and, as such, may be evicted by the stewards at the chairman's order. Nor is this fact of tenancy the sole point which may legally assist the chairman.

Advertisement of Meetings.—Every meeting is called in one of several ways. It may be advertised in the newspapers and other periodicals, summoned by circular, announced by posters and handbills, paragraphed in the Press, or announced by the B.B.C. In short, whatever publicity experience may dictate or ingenuity suggest may be resorted to. But in certain events, especially when there is reason to fear disturbance, the word "Public" should be omitted from the announcements, whatever their form. In this way the promoters will secure their own rights and make clear the exact position of the audience beyond possibility of misapprehension, if they simply drop the word "Public" from every announcement of their meeting. Thus an advertisement of a meeting in favour of the "Reform of Parliament," or to denounce the "Closing of Churches on Week days," will serve every purpose of the promoters, while the omission of the superfluous word "Public" will leave both formalists and rowdies without a legal leg to stand on. If someone has been invited beforehand to preside, as is almost invariably done, the name of the chairman should also appear in the announcement. This will show that he at least has a prescriptive right to occupy the position he holds. Should it turn out that he cannot attend, owing to ill-health or other reason, and there is no time to publish his substitute's name beforehand, the promoters should still be provided with their own chairman; and the secretary will announce to the meeting that Mr. Blank has been appointed to preside in lieu of Mr. So-and-so, whose letter of regret he may (if it is thought right or worth while) read to the audience.

Disturbances.—Notwithstanding the taking of every precaution some evilly-disposed person or persons may make a more or less desperate effort to provoke disturbance of a serious character. One person can be effectually dealt with, and in his case need not be further considered. Grave disorder certainly points to the operations of a gang, who have either been hired for the purpose or, out of some motive of malice or revenge, have decided upon concerted action.

At a remarkable gathering in the Royal Albert Hall, London, some years ago, presided over by Mrs. Henry Fawcett, one of the resolutions was proposed by a well-known Labour M.P. The moment he rose he was assailed by shouts of one kind and another from various parts of the building, by cads who were base enough to jeopardise the success of the meeting by venting their spite and spleen on the speaker. The authorities had evidently anticipated that some such outbreak was on the *tapis*, for handbills were at once circulated throughout the vast throng:—"TAKE NO NOTICE: DO NOT LOOK ROUND." The speaker stood to his guns—it was essential he should do so—and said everything he desired to say. Pauses, of course, were numerous, for it was useless to "crack" his voice against the yells of the mob; but by getting in a sentence now and again in the lulls and biding his time, he wore down the bulk of the crazy shouters and finished his speech triumphantly. As soon as he sat down the audience rose to their feet and acclaimed him with rounds of cheers. Then the organist, grasping the situation, played "For he's a jolly good fellow," which the immense multitude sang with great gusto. Here was an example of riot defeating itself. The would-be creators of dissension had only succeeded in provoking an extraordinary demonstration in favour of the object of their hatred and malice. Was Mrs. Fawcett dismayed? Not in the least. She calmly reviewed the exciting scene and allowed the storm to spend itself. This was, in such a place on such an occasion, the wisest thing to do; but had the number of malcontents been larger it is evident that the meeting would have been wrecked, unless the M.P. had bent before the storm. This he could not have done without imminent damage to his career.

We might multiply instances of riotous demonstrations against certain persons, but for whose presence meetings would have been not only completely successful, but wholly peaceable. In such circumstances the promoters, of course, could not throw the speakers to the wolves, and, what is more, the speakers would not have suffered it.

The Chairman's Warning.—Disturbances, however, are, generally speaking, aimed less at persons than at the objects for which the meeting is being held and, in such cases, are infinitely more easy to deal with, the venomous and vitriolic element being absent. Where a disturbance of this sort breaks out, the chairman should remind the audience that the meeting has been summoned by certain persons for a well-defined and legitimate purpose; that these persons being sole lessees of the premises, all others are present only by permission, which will be withdrawn from anyone whatever causing disturbance or annoying others; that such offenders will not be tolerated, but warned off the premises and, on refusal, will be treated as trespassers and forcibly ejected. In making his statement the chairman must be short, sharp, and to the point; he must not betray anger even if he feel it; and on no account must he employ threatening language or use words which might augment the existing tension and precipitate uproar. These cautionary sentences may or may not have the required result. He must "wait and see." If, however, they prove of no avail, he shall then proceed to name or point out any disorderly person, bid him leave and, if necessary, order him to be turned out.

Stewards.—Eviction, obviously, cannot be carried out by the chairman, but he is not helpless on that account. "Coming events cast their shadows before," and so, as we said, rumours of premeditated trouble usually reach the ears of the "powers that be." There is only one way of meeting a difficulty of that nature. The truth of the reports must be taken for granted: to hesitate at this stage is to be lost. A few days beforehand the promoters must enrol a body of stewards, the number of whom will depend upon the circumstances of the case. For a small meeting a score of men will suffice; for a gathering of imposing dimensions a small army of volunteers—at least five per cent. of the expected attendance—will be required. The word "volunteers" is used advisedly; they are probably personally interested in the meeting, and are likely to be much more intelligent than mercenaries. They should be thoroughly coached in their duties and in the legal rights of the promoters, whose servants they virtually are for the time being. Needless to add, they ought to be strong, sturdy fellows, and of exceptionally good temper and very patient. A captain should be chosen (by the men themselves) for every company of twenty, and they ought to be distinguished by a conspicuous badge labelled "Steward," so that it may be known to all and sundry, that they act under authority. No matter how sympathetic the audience may be—and it is practically certain that, barring the disturbers of the peace, they will support the promoters —the task of quelling disorder should be left to the stewards. They are protected by law in what they do, so long as they use no more force than is absolutely necessary in ejecting a rioter, but a private person might conceivably render himself liable to an action for assault and battery. The captains, each of whom will carry a whistle of peculiar *timbre*, will post their men in selected parts of the hall. Probably a well-disposed array of such maintainers of order will of itself hold the rowdy element in check. Should it be necessary to act, however, they must frankly tell misbehavers that, if they do not cease their annoyance, leave to be present will be cancelled and they will be turned out as trespassers. This unpleasant business should be carried out in a workmanlike manner, with the use of as little force as possible. Where offenders lose their heads and are guilty of undoubted violence, they must be "run out," and should the case be very bad, given into the custody of the police. The stewards should observe the faces of the men they handle, and, when they reach the vestibule, obtain, if they can, their names and addresses, in the event of legal proceedings being afterwards taken. Throughout the meeting, they should act, as far as may be, under the direction of the chairman, but as his eye cannot penetrate the recesses of a huge assembly, independent action, under the guidance of their captains, must not be shirked. The captains, of course, will use their whistles (to summon the aid of another company) only in the last resort.

The Police.—We have purposely selected an example of the worst type of disorder, that of a prearranged effort on a wide scale to upset the business of an enormous meeting, because milder cases can be dealt with by a modification of the procedure sketched. Allusion was made in the last paragraph to the police. The presence of two or three constables is commonly solicited as a matter of course at most meetings, even when they promise to be the calmest and best-behaved. But whenever disturbance may reasonably be expected an adequate body of police should be secured by the promoters. If the circumstances are laid before the authorities, they may be left to take the necessary steps, and will send a sufficient body of men to preserve the peace and protect law-abiding citizens. Any person who has wilfully created disorder may be taken into custody on one of three counts, or perhaps on all three, namely, for obstructing the police in the discharge of their duty; for assault; and for deliberate destruction of property. As to obstruction, the constable may act on his own initiative, and, preferably, should do so. In the other two cases, a steward may give the offender into custody. Save in extreme provocation, however, he ought to be satisfied with getting the culprit outside the building and preventing his return. Constables differ, and some decline to interfere until a breach of the peace really occurs; yet it is their duty to prevent breaches and they should at least be required to do so much. However, should a blow be actually struck they will hardly refrain from action, because it is then their imperative duty to exercise their powers, and, in the event of their refusing to act, their numbers should be taken and they should be reported for neglect of duty. Speaking generally, and having regard to the inherent difficulties, it is seldom advisable to go as far as a summons for illegal conduct at a meeting. Expulsion, as a rule, may be held to meet the offence. Only an absolutely clear case will justify a steward either in giving a culprit into custody or in summoning him. A spirit of vindictiveness is easily aroused, and much trouble may ensue by an action for false imprisonment, which might or might not succeed, but which anyhow would involve both anxiety and expense. The expulsion of disorderly persons will be all that is needed in the vast majority of cases, and the chairman, promoters, and stewards may rest satisfied in having, to that extent, vindicated the right of meeting without let or hindrance.

CHAPTER XIII

THE SOCIAL CHAIRMAN.

The Dinner Chairman.—We have written a great deal concerning the "Company" chairman, the chairman of a meeting, and the president of a board; but though these do not exhaust the business activities of Mr. Chairman, it is time we considered him in his social aspect, as, for instance, a dinner chairman.

As compared with the business chairman the social chairman can win more kudos as a speaker, his office permitting the display of the most varied gifts, and if the reader cares to study a little volume which can be strongly recommended,* he will find in it hints, and the framework of after-dinner and other speeches.

The dinner chairman should not go to the function weary or worried. He should, if possible, put aside the business cares which have oppressed him during the day, and attend to his pleasant duties without any disturbing thought. He will then be able to display the cheerfulness which is so desirable in one who has to be at the head of a sociable company throughout a long evening.

Arrangements.—It is essential that the details in connection with the dinner should be adjusted several days before. The chairman may lend the committee the benefit of his experience, and, in any case, will communicate to the secretary any matter respecting which he is personally interested, such as the guests (if any) and the toast list. There are secretaries *and* secretaries, and unfortunately some of these officers are past-masters in the art of procrastination. The chairman, therefore, must give the secretary clearly to understand that every detail, even to the most

* "Speeches and Toasts" (Published by Ward, Lock & Co., Ltd.)

minute, must be attended to and finally disposed of before the eventful evening. It is manifestly unfair to the chairman to leave one or more matters of moment until the last. The chairman is entitled to more consideration than is usually paid to him.

Before the guests take their places there should be printed and distributed complete programmes of the after-dinner proceedings, giving a list of all the toasts, with their proposers and responders, and of the musical items to come between them. It is a help to less ready speakers if a musical number is inserted between the proposal of a toast, and the response.

Duty to Guests.—The chairman should see that his guests are properly seated with reference to himself, and it is as well, in smaller gatherings particularly, that he should be acquainted with the names and standing, both social and commercial, of those around him. Thus informed by the secretary, the chairman will be enabled to say the few words to the guests and others which show him to be a man of the world and familiar with the position and other attributes (on which comment is thus allowable) of his varied guests. A judicious compliment, a happy epithet, will go far to put him on terms even with the strangers who may be present.

This knowledge may be of further service to the chairman in the course of the evening, for during one or other of his speeches, he may make a hit by an apt reference to some of those at table. The less apparent are the efforts in the direction of gaining this knowledge, the better. Any whispered queries, or louder inquiry, sent round as regards the identity of some well-known person may meet his ears, and will not sound pleasantly.

It is, therefore, most desirable that the chairman should know not only who is actually present, but who is who and which is which. Informed of this beforehand he will not have to ask the otherwise inevitable questions, and thus will escape offending those who are tenacious of recognition.

In addition to "who" and "what" the chairman needs to know "where."

Plan of Dinner-Table.—It is a manifest convenience (more readily appreciable at large dinners where the attendance exceeds one or perhaps two hundred persons) to have pre-

G

pared beforehand a plan of the dinner-tables, on which the place of every guest is marked. The secretary had better attend to the drawing-up of the plan. It will cost him some trouble, but the saving of confusion and crushing which it effects will repay him. The plan may either be printed (a copy being given to every diner, with his own name underlined in red, or otherwise distinguished) or, if it exist only in MS., in the form of a large-scale sketch, it should be exhibited on an easel in the reception-room, where each diner may study it and ascertain exactly where he will find his place.

Besides the obvious advantage of being in possession of a key to the board before him, and being able by its means to examine the composition of the tables, the chairman and his guests are, in a fashion, introduced to each other, and conversation may at once be started without risk of *faux pas*.

It is very often judicious for a chairman, if of high standing, or a great favourite, to refer in his speech to my friend Mr. So-and-So, who is seated at "such a table." The person thus honoured and selected for mention will be the more pleased if his acquaintance with the chairman is really slight! The table-plan has thus an advantage which the judicious chairman will seize.

Toastmaster.—At important banquets the chairman is customarily assisted by a functionary who, though styled "toastmaster," has to make every announcement which the chairman desires to place before the company. It is, however, more in consonance with the claims of hospitality when the chairman, who occupies the position of host, discharges all the duties of the post. It is more becoming and more gracious for the chairman, rather than a hireling, to play the host. Consequently, should the chairman feel equal to fulfilling all the duties which he would perform (as a matter of course) in his own house, he ought certainly to fulfil them at a public dinner. In that case he should instruct the secretary to intimate to the manager of the hotel or assembly rooms where the dinner is to be held that the services of a toastmaster will not be required.

"Grace."—The chairman having seen his guests seated at his side, and the company in their places, will either request the toastmaster to call "Grace," or, if no such functionary is

present, will himself ask the chaplain or some other clergyman or minister to say "Grace," the company standing. This preliminary duty performed—perhaps by the chairman himself—the company are seated, and dinner is served.

Dinner Duties.—While the dinner is in progress the chairman will, of course, naturally concentrate his attention upon his immediate neighbours, who may be either his own guests or the more distinguished visitors who have been invited to attend as the guests, it may be, of the institution or club which is giving the dinner. It is the chairman's prerogative to show especial courtesy to guests who are exceptionally favoured.

An ideal chairman will know the subject best calculated to discover his neighbour's confidence. He will assail him with the topic he best understands, or is most acquainted with, being, moreover, mindful to avoid controversial questions, unless he is absolutely sure of his man. A mistake in this regard will not readily be forgiven.

Subjects Tabooed.—As a general rule in social gatherings politics and religion are avoided. To introduce either is considered to be tantamount to casting a firebrand into the "haggart," and the flame quickly spreads if fanned. Let the judicious chairman, therefore, avoid both politics and religion.

Smaller Functions.—The same general rule should apply also to the chairman of a small club-dinner, although the smaller the gathering the more difficult it is to entertain. Each one is more or less shy in beginning the conversation, or in making it general. Hence the party is broken up at once into its component parts. Each man who is seated next to an acquaintance turns to and converses with him, perhaps, in a low tone, while the solitary diner sits dumb, crumbling his bread, or reading for the hundredth time the "Menu," which he is probably heartily tired of ere he is half through it prandially.

The chairman should endeavour to allay this uneasiness. Knowing, perhaps, that the solitary diner has a hobby, the chairman may (addressing him by name) question him concerning it, and then by involving the stranger's neighbour in the discussion informally introduce them to one another.

The chairman will now be at ease and, having set "the ball rolling" and made all comfortable, may permit the conversation to flow past him, if he chooses, and let his *convives* assist him.

As Host.—In this as in other respects the chairman should play the host rather than the president, and be chary of asserting his personality and of expressing his opinions too strongly, or of dominating the conversation. If called upon to relate an anecdote, let him do so, but he should try to promote the harmony and the sociability of the company generally, rather than to assert himself, except in those duties which, as chairman, he must carry out.

Even in the social gatherings of small clubs which meet infrequently, and at which the members may be comparative strangers, it is fortunately the case that there are usually one or two persons who are disposed to conversation, and who purposely cast a scrap of debatable matter of an innocuous character before them. On this morsel some guest eagerly pounces, and then, like so many hens, the others rush after the fortunate one, anxious to peck at the controversial morsel with him. Thus dullness is dissipated and geniality introduced in its stead.

"Taking Wine."—We will suppose the dinner progressing. At a certain time, fairly early in the proceedings, the chairman takes wine with the company. (The phrase "takes wine" is more or less conventional. The chairman may be a strict abstainer and take nothing stronger than ginger ale, yet he will not refrain from using the time-honoured formula.)

If the gathering is small, and most of the guests on friendly terms, the chairman will convey a hint to one of his neighbours, who rises and says:—

"Gentlemen [or Brother Members], the chairman will be pleased to take wine with you."

The company respond, standing up, and the chairman seats himself and the conversation is renewed.

But at large dinners the toastmaster gives the word: "Gentlemen to the right of the Chair, the Chairman [or his Lordship] will take wine with you."

The chairman rises, bows to the right, and the guests on his right respond; and so in turn, shortly afterwards, he will show similar courtesy to those on his left. Ordinarily this "taking wine" with the company is the only duty of the chairman during dinner.

Other categories will suggest themselves. For example, at a "firm" dinner the chairman (who is usually the employer) will take wine in turn with each of the various departments, counting-house, export, selling, administrative, etc., thereby suggesting to the employees that he is in touch with each of them and that no good work passes unnoticed. It will be well for him to have a list prepared; the accidental omission of one department would be unfortunate and might even seem invidious. The "taking wine" formula has possibilities of humour and chaff which must be resisted at large and formal gatherings, although useful in promoting hilarity on more riotous occasions, such as annual dinners of football and cricket clubs. "The chairman will take wine with the members who have not dropped a catch during the season" will set tongues wagging. But these relaxations should be thought out beforehand, in order that they may be kept free of offence.

Toasts, etc.—After dinner the duties of the chairman begin in earnest with the toast of "The King." A soloist will perhaps sing a verse of the National Anthem, the company joining in the chorus, and when the toast has been duly honoured—not before—the chairman gives permission to smoke.

As to the loyal toast, the chairman should note that the better plan is merely to give it (after a full pause for general attention) in the simple words "The King." The loyal toast should precede all other functions of the after-dinner.

One innovation we once witnessed which appeared to meet with general approval. The chairman on the occasion in question was a former Lord Provost of Edinburgh, and his experience at civic functions must have satisfied him that there was nothing really improper in the practice he initiated. After the sweets and during the dessert he rose from his seat as chairman and gave the toast of "The King." The result was that those who wished to dally over the fruit could do so, while those who desired to smoke could, for after the loyal toast had been duly honoured, the chairman gave permission, by consent of the ladies present, to smoke.

Ladies Present.—When ladies are present at a dinner, this fact must alter the very first words, and it must also qualify some of the sanctions of the chair. For instance, after the loyal toast at a dinner, leave to smoke is granted; but when ladies attend the function intimation must run somewhat to this effect,—"Gentlemen, I am happy to announce that by gracious permission of the ladies, smoking may now be indulged in." It will be observed that this notice is adroitly framed. Under its terms all men may smoke also those ladies who care to. And, by the by, at this same after-dinner entertainment, if ladies are to be present, let the chairman satisfy himself beforehand that there will be no equivocal stories or suggestive and vulgar songs. This hint is not thrown out idly, or without experience of unpleasant moments. In these days of women's activities their presence may be looked for at all kinds of gatherings, and they are doubtless accustomed to take the risks inseparable from some meetings; but they should never be exposed to malice aforethought or the ribald *double entendre.*

Duty Toasts.—This brings us to the question of the toasts which it is the chairman's duty to propose. They, of course, vary in number, according to the place and the occasion. Generally they number three—"The King and Royal Family"; the Toast of the Evening, which may be "Prosperity." to the institution or club; and "The Guests of the Evening"; though the last is often relegated to another member.

To these may be added others, as may be deemed necessary; but the chairman is usually more than content with three and with "returning thanks" for the Toast of his own health. In some cases the "(Lord) Mayor and Sheriffs," or the "(Lord) Provost and Bailies," and other functionaries must be separately toasted. "The Vicar," "the County [or other] Members," "the Churchwardens," "the Army and Navy," "the Air Force," or "the Territorial Army," and other toasts may be proposed by the chairman, if the function is local, and a "heavy" programme is preferred.

Again, "the Houses of Parliament," "the Bishop and Clergy of the Diocese," "His Majesty's Ministers," "His Majesty's Judges," "the Lord-Lieutenant," "Magistrates," and other dignitaries may have to be toasted upon many and various occasions by the chairman of public and semi-public dinners and banquets.

Chairman's Characteristics.—To perform these duties satisfactorily he must be a man of resource, and must not repeat himself—nor must he be too lengthy in his remarks. Prolixity is fatal to the chairman of a dinner. He must seize the essentials of his subject, hold them, discuss them briefly, not wandering far afield and losing himself so completely as to be unable subsequently to find his way back to his proper theme.

The chairman should, therefore, write his speech out, and con it at home, and, having the notes of it before him, or in his head, deliver it, with such occasional comment and elucidation as may seem demanded by the degree of receptivity of his audience. With an inexperienced speaker this added matter may be absolutely necessary if the argument is to be followed. The written speech may have the qualities of good writing rather than those of good speaking, and be too closely knit to be taken in at a hearing. Oratory demands emphasis, and, in places, repetition. The maker of a prepared speech, although he be inexperienced, may have intuition, and be able to feel when what he is saying does not "get across" and therefore needs amplification. Practice makes perfect, and he may soon be able to speak with ease after no more preparation than a writing down of the heads of his intended address. But men are not all alike in this respect. Some of the most practised speakers prepare very fully.

Humour is generally appreciated in a chairman; lightness of touch (whenever the subject admits of it) and sympathy (always) tell admirably with the listeners.

The chairman must keep his eyes open, and exercise his authority whenever it may be called for—in commanding silence, in keeping the waiters out of the room, if necessary, in arranging the programme, and announcing, or calling upon, the artistes to sing or play. All these are important points, and he will take care also to name those present who are connected with any toast he may propose.

The chairman will thus name certain of the guests to reply for "the Houses of Parliament," and pursue similar vigilance in supervising the remaining toasts, at least as far as that of "the Guests." When artistes are present the chairman should be careful that someone—if not himself—shall propose a vote of thanks for their services and entertainment. .

These are the principal duties which the dinner chairman must perform. They vary with the occasion; but as ample notice is usually given, the chairman has only a poor excuse —if he accepts the position—for not performing those duties adequately. A chairman should remember that such an invitation is an honour that, if accepted, entails responsibilities that should be rigorously carried out.

Non-Attendance.—To send an excuse at the last moment, unless it be quite valid, is a gross insult to the expectant company, and should be resented. The person guilty of such egregiously bad form would probably be the first—being a selfish person—to complain if some one else threw him over. A golden rule is, "If you promise, perform, unheeding personal inconvenience."

Punctuality.—Then, again, punctuality is a virtue everywhere, but nowhere more essential than at dinners. The busiest men are always the most punctual. Your *quasi*-busy man is frequently late, because he procrastinates, and permits interference with his time. There are, of course, cases when breaking a promise is unavoidable; but an engagement made many days before is like a special train; the lines should be clear for it, and it should keep time right royally. To be later than the generally ample margin provided is bad taste, and rude. Unpunctuality throws out the arrangements, and tends to spoil the dinner. The temper of those kept waiting is not improved either; so the chairman who is regardful of his popularity will not keep his *convives* waiting.

Reception.—As host it is the duty of the chairman to be present in time to receive every guest. It is little short of a scandal how perfunctorily this duty is frequently performed. Over and over again half of the company arrives before the chairman, and, in such circumstances, how can the welcome he tenders be anything but a farce? The guests wander aimlessly about the room set apart for their reception, and when the defaulting chairman at last arrives, hardly one of them deems it worth while to go out of the room to make a formal entry. And we cannot be surprised at this. It is incredible that, were the chairman entertaining friends at a dinner-party in his house, he would make his appearance after most of his guests had arrived. He should treat a company of comparative strangers (as the bulk of them must necessarily be) with courtesy at least equal to that which he would show in private life. But for the convenience of a rendezvous where they might all meet, the reception might, in many instances, be abandoned, and guests proceed directly from the cloak-room to the dining salon. Such an innovation would deal a deadly blow at public dinners. Every chairman should cultivate the duty of scrupulous punctuality.

Assistance.—We have supposed the chairman to make himself acquainted with all the necessary details; but the stewards, or in some cases the secretary, will supply any information. The chairman should therefore always have an office-bearer (preferably the secretary) within call—one who will supply any information he may require, or who will post him in details, if necessary, and communicate to the respondents to the various toasts the duties expected of them.

Speeches.—As regards speeches, this is hardly the place in which to discuss or detail them, but examples for various occasions will be given in a later chapter. We can only suggest that the chairman should, as a general rule, be brief and to the point. Of course, in certain circumstances, brevity is not wit, nor the soul thereof. A special subject may demand breadth of treatment and elaboration, but for how long the chairman should speak to it will depend upon many factors. Lord Birkenhead or Dean Inge would be given *carte blanche* for an after-dinner speech, where five minutes from an unqualified person would be too much. On ordinary occasions a bright, happy, unpretentious speech of from five to ten minutes will suffice for a leading toast. The others can be despatched in four or five minutes each with perfect propriety, with justice to themselves and to the speech-maker.

CHAPTER XIV

ON THE CHOICE OF A CHAIRMAN.

A Look Round.—From a consideration of the manifold duties which the office of chairman embraces, it is apparent that it will not be easy to discover men who are competent to discharge all of them with equal efficiency. Nor, in point of fact, will such a quest ever be necessary. For though we have discussed many varied functions between the boards of this volume, it is most improbable that any one person will be asked to act as chairman of meetings of more than three or four different kinds. A mayor, or provost, or chairman of a council—county, town, district, or urban—may, in virtue of his office and during his term of office, have to preside over diverse gatherings; but his case is entirely exceptional. Nor, so far as his own chair is concerned, will there be any difficulty in selecting a suitable man to fill it, since the choice is vested in his fellow-members, and they have ample opportunities for observing ability and general qualifications for the post on the part of their brethren. We have rather to deal with the more complicated question of the occasional chairman who may hold office for a period or only for a single meeting.

The Well-to-do Man.—There is a natural tendency to look to men of good social standing, prosperous, and with plenty of leisure, to play a prominent part in local affairs. Frequently something more than compliment is intended by the choice of a man in what are called "easy circumstances." It is hoped a *quid pro quo* may be forthcoming in the shape of a substantial cheque, a handsome prize, or other gift. Other things being equal, there may be no harm in placing a wealthy person in the chair; though it must not be assumed that when money is wanted for a worthy object, it can only be had by dangling a social reward before the eyes of a likely patron. Human nature is a great deal better than some cynics imagine, and a man will often give of his abundance merely from a wish to render service, without further thought. For many reasons it is unwise to install a rich man in office simply because he *is* rich. Not only may he assume an equivalent share of power, but if he spends money freely to curry favour, he may frighten off, as possible successors to himself, poor, able men who might have made most acceptable chairmen. It is extremely easy to draw up a list of the qualities one expects in an ideal chairman, but it will be practically impossible to find them embodied in one man. We must be content, therefore, if he possess some of the more essential of them; but it is certain that wealth alone is not a sufficient qualification. In this connection, however, the advice of Tennyson's Northern Farmer to his son recurs to one: "Don't thou marry for munny, but goa wheer munny is."

The Capable Man.—But rich or poor, the first desideratum is a man in heart-whole sympathy with the object of the society or the meeting. The value of genuine, well-disciplined enthusiasm cannot be stated in terms of money, and if an enthusiast of that sort, as distinguished from a sentimentalist, can be found willing to accept office, let his name go forward for nomination at once. And when you get him, keep him. The rules of the society may require every office-bearer to be elected annually. Such a regulation is salutary, but take care that this jewel of a chairman, like the phœnix, shall rise again from his ashes. Emphasis is laid upon this, not without reason.

" *Let the Honours Go Round.*"—For there is a poor, trumpery saying that is frequently trotted out at annual meetings and works an incredible amount of mischief. On these occasions the man with a grievance is sure to be in evidence. He objects to this and that and talks vaguely of "fresh blood." Having mounted his hobby the busybody gives it full rein, and ere he comes to a stop once more he usually succeeds in quickening the sluggish pulse of men of similarly narrow views. Thus when the question of appointing a chairman is reached, and the proposal to re-elect the tried and true man is made, he is ready with his protest. "Let the honours go round," is his favourite maxim. Claptrap wears a specious look, and, if the soberer spirits do not hold the hot heads in check, a snatched victory may be gained and a rank duffer installed in office for a year, with detrimental results. Of course, seriously considered, the advice will not bear examination, and should be disregarded as the idle exhortation of a splenetic malcontent. When a society or a committee is so lucky as to secure a good man for any post, let it do its level best to keep him. When it has the misfortune to be served with a weak one, let it release him from office without delay. It is absolutely true that no man is indispensable, but when you have the conjunction of the man and the post, or the post and the man, do not be so foolish as to seek to dissolve the union. Nor is it by any means a healthy sign when business offices come to be coveted as "honours." It is to be hoped that it may always be esteemed both an honour and a privilege to fill the position of chairman; yet let it not be supposed that the post is a sinecure carrying no important business duties, else it may in time (and perhaps soon rather than later) cease to be regarded as an honour. However, when, owing to some deplorable blunder, the round peg has been put in the square hole, the sooner the mischief is undone the better.

The Everyday Chairman.—But chairmen of the highest class are not as thick as blackberries, and when a man of this order is not to be had, the services of the next best must be secured—and these, happily, are not so far to seek. When a man is approached with a view to occupancy of the office, too much weight need not be attached to the disclaimer of fitness which modesty may dictate. He must be assured of a reasonable amount of co-operation and the confidence of his colleagues must be generous. Thus backed he will soon acquire self-reliance, and a diligent study of this book will put him in possession of a knowledge of the technical minutiæ of his post. The promises of assistance held out to him in order to induce him to serve must not be kept to the ear and broken to the hope. The secretary must be loyal and play the game. The two should arrange to meet half an hour before business and go over the agenda together, since the chairman can know nothing of the details which pass through the secretary's hands. The sight of a chairman idly turning over papers and (foolishly) answering questions at a venture may and does discredit him, but it also conveys an imputation of neglect of duty which the secretary may find it difficult to answer satisfactorily. Granted, on the other hand, cordial collaboration between the two office-holders, the average chairman will more frequently than not develop into a capable president and, in time, the work will fascinate him.

The Working-Man in the Chair.—In many industrial districts it will often happen that a working-man will be invited to assist in movements for the common good; nor is this unlikely even in truly rural areas. There is nothing connected with the duties of a chairman which an intelligent working-man cannot readily master, and since agencies for the public welfare, in most of which the interests of labour are involved, are increasing, it follows that a decided advantage is gained by securing the co-operation of working-men and women, many of whom, moreover, have distinguished themselves by a special study of economic subjects.

Specialization.—In these days when specialization is universal, it is not surprising that some attempt is made to place in the chair specialists in the particular subject to be discussed.   No doubt it is exceedingly helpful to have an expert in the chair of, say, a committee on tuberculosis; but there he sits, not *quà* chairman, but because of his unique knowledge and experience of the subject under investigation. Indeed, it is quite conceivable that, as chairman, this specialist might not be nearly so competent as a layman whose opinion on consumption has no value whatever. A specialist who is also an experienced chairman is the ideal man for the position; but, failing this, one accustomed to control meetings but with no expert knowledge of the matter in hand will do better than a scientific authority ignorant of commitee and public-meeting procedure.

Women in the Chair.—It is characteristic of the age that women are not shirking their share of the public life of the community. They are members of every kind of board, society, and committee, and now occupy several seats in the House of Commons. If it is conceded that they are capable of filling the mayoral chair, and of presiding over all manner of social organisations, there is no reason whatever why their services should not be systematically retained to discharge duties ordinarily regarded as the prerogative of man. As has been mentioned in another chapter of this book, the late Mrs. Henry Fawcett many years ago presided over a monster meeting in the Royal Albert Hall, London, and proved herself equal to a crisis the like of which has tested the nerve and steadiness of men, who have not always emerged from their "baptism of fire" so smilingly as did Mrs. Fawcett. Undoubtedly, sex counts for something, and there is a natural tendency, in circumstances when no mercy would be shown to man, to let woman down gently. So far as that makes for decency of manners in public discussion it is all to the good. Therefore the presence of women in the chair is to be encouraged rather than deprecated. The title of "Chairman" appears not to be resented. Doubtless, "chairwoman," in the mouths of many persons of affected pronunciation, would approximate too near to "charwoman" to render its use in meetings and elsewhere at all desirable. Of course, any difficulty that might be felt on the score of accuracy could readily be got over by employing the surname instead. The lady already alluded to could hardly object to a man beginning his remarks "Mrs. Fawcett," and interpolating "Madam," where, in other and less happy moments, he would employ "Sir."

An Incompetent Chairman.—Queen Elizabeth, happening to meet Sir John Popham one day, inquired of him "what had passed in the Lower House." The Speaker laconically answered, "Seven weeks, if it please your Majesty," the implication being that the Commons had sat for that length of time without transacting any business. The story illustrates, in another respect, of course (for no reflection is meant on Mr. Speaker Popham), the folly of permitting a hopelessly incapable person to occupy the chair. Readers will be better able to appreciate the intolerable annoyance which this may occasion by a brief description of the course of a meeting held within a hundred miles of the City of London, for the purpose of considering a social project of no small importance. There was a good attendance, as might have been anticipated, but when the hour struck at which the proceedings ought to have begun no chairman had appeared. Some "law" was allowed him in case of accidental detention through no fault of his own; but time in the capital of the British Empire is precious, and the audience grew weary of waiting. The promoters of the meeting seeming to be panic-stricken, one gentleman after another was proposed for the post, but every nominee (for reasons which it was obviously impossible to verify and which, therefore, had to be accepted) declined to serve.

The situation was rapidly becoming farcial when, to the general relief, someone at length offered to officiate. Alas, the gentleman of good intent turned out to be altogether unequal to his self-assumed task. He committed blunders innumerable, thankfully received the smallest contributions of advice from various members of the audience, now grown dictatorial, and plunged the meeting into a condition of chaos, out of which it was only delivered by a few level-headed men who, for decency's sake and without much regard to form, got the business through somehow. The muddle might have been invented to show the necessity for a book such as this, as well as to demonstrate the prudence of men and women, interested in public affairs, possessing at least a bowing acquaintance with the routine of conducting a meeting in an intelligent, businesslike, and orderly fashion. It is to be feared, however, that the call of duty finds too many men and women unready. Holding, as we do, that a lively sense of public spirit is not only commendable in itself but ought to be encouraged, we suggest that a good citizen, when urged by letter or deputation to place himself at the head of a committee, society, or meeting, of the *raison d'être* of which he personally approves, should consent, and qualify himself for the labours which acceptance of office will entail.

Personal.—In reviewing the subject of chairmanship, let us see what we have learned. For committee work—where aptitude is more material than brilliancy—it is not at all necessary that the chairman should be a good speaker: indeed, a man who likes to hear the sound of his own voice may become a nuisance. Though it is preposterous to rush business, as is sometimes done under the totally erroneous impression that hustle is now the accepted hall-mark of a man of affairs, it is equally culpable to hang it up by endless talk over things that do not count, with the result that really essential matters are scamped from sheer weariness. The model chairman should speak his mind in a few clear, pointed, and appropriate sentences, and then endeavour to induce his colleagues to be equally precise. Guidance and control are the desiderata in the chairman of a committee, but they presuppose a man of tact, judgment, and genial temper, possessed of the knack or gift of coming, if need be, to a sound decision on the spur of the moment. These qualitites may appear rare, but they will be discerned if matters are not hurried on unduly at the beginning. A good start does not necessarily mean a premature start. Take time to get the right man in the right place, for the success of a movement, or a meeting, may be assured forthwith, because a man of known weight and influence has consented to take the chair. *Per contra*, a committee may be hampered from its very inception—no matter how unexceptionable the object for which it exists—simply because the leadership of the obvious man was not secured. Punctuality and despatch are of real moment in committee work. The busiest man has most time because he has reduced the utilisation of time to a fine art. He attends every meeting and begins business at the minute. If he is lax, he will find the members grow equally slack. If he misses a meeting now and then, he loses touch with the affairs of the committee, labours under a disadvantage, and his usefulness is impaired. One cannot altogether replace first-hand knowledge even if carefully posted up by an industrious secretary. Eye and ear observe things which cannot always be noted by the pen. As stated in cold print, the factors that go to the choice of a competent chairman may not seem easy of attainment, but it is nevertheless always and everywhere true that "the hour finds the man."

CHAPTER XV

TYPICAL SPEECHES FROM THE CHAIR.

Short Speeches.—One of several respects in which Mr. Chairman differs from his colleagues is that he is not expected to deliver long speeches. He may have to speak often, but he seldom has to speak at length. The main reason for this is that he is not only the figure-head of the gathering he presides over, but its business head also. When, as sometimes happens, the chief speech at a meeting or at a dinner falls to the lot of the chairman, this will invariably be found to be due to the fact that he is a man occupying a pre-eminent position in politics, art, literature, science, music, drama, commerce, industry, or other sphere of human thought and enterprise. Men of such distinction are exceptions. The average chairman, for whom this book is mainly intended, is not pre-eminent in any walk of life. For him it is wise frankly to recognise that he is the manager of the meeting, that his function is the useful. That is why the part is so frequently given to a man of affairs. Enjoying the exercise of power, and attracted rather than daunted by the responsibility it involves, he is content, having the substance, to leave the appearance to others. The exercise of control is what he really likes, and, for this, much speaking is merely waste of time.

It is not suggested that he is necessarily without ability as a speaker, but that he conceives his speeches on totally different lines from those adopted by orators. His aim is not eloquence but brevity, crispness, lucidity. He will not eschew humour nor shun anecdote, but he will compress what he has to say into a few minutes, while others may run to ten or fifteen minutes and sometimes even longer. But because brevity is the brand of the chairman, he must neither be hurried nor flurried. He must be easy, deliberate, and comfortable, and if he can wear a smiling face (unless the dividend is down or missing), so much the better. He must not shout or pitch his voice too high. The acoustics of many rooms are exceedingly trying, but when he finds his voice come back to him readily he will know that he is on his right note. A chairman is more effective as a speaker when his remarks appear to be *ex tempore*, and he should at all events avoid reading his speeches. It will be quite proper to make a few memoranda of all that he must say—in fact, this is to be recommended, lest he may forget some important point. When he has occasion to speak at length, as now and again happens, he should certainly think over what he intends to speak about : he may even find it useful to commit the whole of the speech to paper and afterwards to memory. This presupposes coolness and presence of mind, for a foolish question or frivolous interruption may cause him to lose his thread and, in such predicament, his last state may be decidedly worse than his first.

In submitting a few typical speeches, it must be understood that they will serve only as patterns. Even as patterns they are necessarily imperfect. All speeches "in the air" must be. What gives life to a speech, sometimes to even an otherwise poor speech, is the happiness or sincerity of the local allusions. This charity club, association, is not just one of a class. It has a special appeal to you, or presumably you would not be presiding at its meetings. Make this special interest clear, speak about what you have at heart as if you had a heart, and you will have your hearers with you. But the generalities of the following speeches will help you to get started, and, what may be even more important, to get finished. But the core of your speech must be the special circumstance of the occasion.

As financial interests loom largely on the horizon of every man who will probably fill the chair, we begin with a speech as chairman.

AT A COMPANY MEETING.

Ladies and Gentlemen,—My first duty is to ask you to receive and adopt the Directors' Report and the Statement of Accounts which accompanies it. You have just decided that they shall be taken as read, and as they have been circulated for some days I venture to assume that you have examined them carefully. I daresay you are disposed to think that the picture which they offer has been painted in sober colours, but it seemed to the Board that the wisest course to pursue was to give a faithful representation of the facts. At the same time, I am satisfied that we are at least holding our own, and that is something to be thankful for in these times of unprecedented hustle and competition, growing keener and keener every year. The position has not varied materially since last we met, and if the dividend is not larger, the figures will show you that at least we have divided all we reasonably could. Whatever unremitting attention to your interests could accomplish has been effected, and I assure you that our General Manager has almost surpassed himself in his efforts to meet the requirements of a concern which demands unceasing vigilance and a trained study of the public taste. Perhaps you may consider that our reserve is unduly large. I would ask you to pause before you counsel any departure from the policy which we have consistently adopted in that particular. Those of you who have been behind the scenes will readily agree with me that a substantial reserve is a pillar of strength to such a company as ours. The Board are resolutely opposed to lavish outlay, on the one hand, and unwise economy on the other, but they will never consent to tamper with the staple features which secure our position financially. There is, in some quarters, a tendency to deprecate care for the future. "Move, act, in the living present," the poet tells us. But you cannot ignore the future, even if you would. We cannot foresee the vicissitudes which a year may bring in trade and commerce, and I hold it to be absolutely incumbent upon the Board never to neglect the reserve.

[*Here, if he chooses, the chairman may pick out a few items from the Report or Accounts, and comment upon them.*]

It is unnecessary that I should detain the meeting any longer. You will hear other aspects of our affairs from the remaining speakers, but should any shareholder desire information upon any point in the Balance Sheet, I hope he will not hesitate to ask such questions as may occur to him. It will be convenient that this should be done before the resolution is put to the vote. Ladies and Gentlemen, I beg formally to move "That the Directors' Report, along with the Balance Sheet as audited, be received and adopted";

and I will request Mr. ——, who, though he has not a seat on the Board, has always manifested a warm interest in the affairs of the Company, to be good enough to second the motion. After that it will be open to anyone to address the meeting.

Before passing on from finance to social functions, the chairman should be reminded that company meetings are often reported at length, and it is important therefore that his facts and figures should be correctly announced. A common custom is for the company to take its own verbatim report which, after revision, may be supplied to the Press.

At a Social Dinner.

Ladies and Gentlemen,—You remember the story of the wee Scottish laddie who was sent to the fishmonger's for a haddock. "Please, sir," he said when he got to the shop, "mither wants a haddie," which is Scots for haddock. "Finnan?" asked the salesman. "No," promptly answered the boy, "a thick 'un." Well, Ladies and Gentlemen, I can only hope that you won't find these remarks of mine a trifle thin. We have met here to enjoy ourselves. We have cast business cares and worries to the winds, and some of us·would be glad to see them no more for ever. It is said, by way of reproach, that we are a pleasure-loving community, far too devoted to sport and frivolity. For my part, Ladies and Gentlemen, I am inclined to plead guilty, but I hope the jury will add, "with extenuating circumstances," and strongly recommend me to mercy. Business is no longer business; it is all that, and a great deal more to boot. The hustle in which we spend our days, and which our worthy fathers had not the ghost of an idea of, absolutely demands a foil, if the breadwinners [*a laugh*] are not to go down to a very premature grave, broken and bruised men, too old at forty. The musical tinkle of a pretty titter fell on my ear just now. I know what the lady is thinking of. She thinks I have mistaken the sex of the breadwinner, that the breadwinner of moral stories is as extinct as the Dodo. She is both right and wrong. The men are still filling a few situations, and I fancy that their lot has not been made any the easier by the competition of their sisters. I may say, therefore, of both sexes, "we are all breadwinners now," but I decline to apply to the charming sex any remark which could be remotely construed as meaning that it could in any circumstances be too old at forty. "Age cannot wither, nor custom stale its infinite variety." But as I do not wish to grow serious— perhaps some may imagine I was born so, but I wasn't—I trust we shall all recognise the wisdom as well as heroism of mixing plenty of pleasure with business. Mirth and happiness are the notes I desire to strike to-night, and if we all do our best to promote the general enjoyment, I believe we shall be none the worse for it in the morning. Nor will work suffer—perish the thought!—because we dedicate these few passing hours to—dare I say?—innocent festivities and jollity, to harmony and hilarity. I am now going to ask you to raise your glasses to our noble selves, for that is what the toast I have to propose comes to. In wishing "Continued success and prosperity to the —— Club," I purposely refrain from dealing with the facts and figures of the past year's history. These belong to our annual meeting, and to-night we hold our annual dinner. The two functions are wholly distinct and separate, and what I have put asunder let no man—nor woman either—dare to join together. Who- ever does so in any speech this evening I shall denounce as a disorderly person. Ladies and Gentlemen,—"Our Club!"

It will be noticed that a blank has been left for the name of the Club. This can be easily filled in. It may be one of those composite bodies which are (fortunately) on the increase, in which the men play bowls or cricket and the girls tennis, not without the co-operation of their male friends, while a few dances and whist drives help to relieve the tedium of winter. Observe, too, that the phrase "a laugh" has actually been interpolated as if the speech were copied from a newspaper report. This is a familiar trick. It may be that a laugh may really be vouchsafed to the chairman at that moment, but if not he must boldly affect that he heard it. The *raconteur* is very fond of the device. He lugs in the word "story" somehow—by the ears, if need be—and then coolly continues—"Talking of stories, that reminds me," and then he is off, full speed ahead.

Almost every man of influence is sure to be invited to take an interest in local affairs, and we will now imagine him in the chair.

At a Meeting of Ratepayers.

Ladies and Gentlemen,—To begin at the beginning, allow me to thank you for the honour you have done me in electing me to the chair to-night. I am glad to be with you in any capacity, for I know no subject of greater importance to the householder than local self-government. Some of you may have read of the old days—now, thank God! gone for ever—of vestries and Bumbledom, when a few by no means disinterested persons were good enough to mismanage our affairs. It was our fault, perhaps, more than theirs. Had we been more public-spirited, many of their malpractices, from some of which we suffer even now, would have been impossible. It was the old story: our indifference was their opportunity. The proverb bids us "Live and learn." That is what we in this room have done, and a pretty price most of us have paid for our lesson. But during the last generation or so there has been an amazing improvement in almost every direction. We demand polls now, and vote, as the joker said, as early and often as we can. The public gallery in our council room is usually well patronized by intelligent hearers, who do not scruple to bestow censure as well as praise—and are sometimes ejected for their trouble. The Press reports our debates at greater length, and the able editor—I believe that is the recognised designation—favours us with occasional articles, apparently too caustic at times for our hard-working councillors. And to-night we are actually holding an indignation meeting because our representatives refuse to tax us! The boot commonly is on the other foot, but here we are met—the poor and the rich, the old and the young—to enter a strong protest against the continued apathy of the council in neglecting to provide a public library. We know that that will cost us money, but the best evidence of our sincerity is, that we demand that a poll of the borough be taken and the feeling of the ratepayers tested. We have reason to suppose that the majority of the council are in conflict with the majority of the people whose votes sent them there. So far as the principle of the matter goes, I am heartily with you. To some extent I confess that I came here to learn, and the speakers who will presently advocate our cause will no doubt enlighten me, together with the rest of the audience. I will just add one or two sentences before proceeding to business. We are painfully aware that our rates are high—too high, in my judgment—and we shall immensely strengthen our case for an additional rate, if some of our freinds address themselves specially to the task of demonstrating how the cost of the equipment and maintenance of a Public Library can be met with no appreciable addition to our burdens. Ladies and Gentlemen, I am anxious that our speaking to-night should be of a representative character, and I trust therefore that intending speakers will keep their remarks as brief as they reasonably can, and each deal with a separate point. In that way I am certain an overwhelming case can be made out for the institution of a public library in our midst; and if the reporters whom I see before me can induce their editors to wield the blue pencil with tender solicitude, I think the sale of next Saturday's papers may reach a record. I call upon Mrs. Constant Reader to propose the first resolution.

With Labour directly represented in every legislative assembly in the British Empire, it is scarcely necessary to say that all artisans and labourers take an intense and intelligent interest in public affairs. Many of them, indeed, are willing and able to assume the duties of chairman.

At a Workmen's Institute.

Ladies and Gentlemen,—In the name of the committee, who have invited me to preside here to-night, I bid one and all a hearty welcome to this meeting. I am happy to see several women in our midst. Well do I know the conditions under which they serve the community, and the difficulties with which they have to contend in their home-life, and it says much for their zeal and self-denial that they have come to show their practical sympathy with us. This institute has done great things for their men and their boys, and their presence is appreciated because it testifies to gratitude for the past and confidence in the future. And that brings me to the subject with which we shall be concerned at this gathering. It has seemed to many of us that wonderful as the success of this institute has been, its work and usefulness have been, if I may so express myself, somewhat lop-sided. What we have achieved hitherto has been for the advantage of the men and lads. We have done nothing as yet for the women. God knows, and you will believe me, it was not for want of will. You see a decently-furnished, prosperous institution, but you are not aware of the uphill job it has been to reach this success, of the weary months and years during which progress was so slow that at times we almost lost heart. We have had to labour and hâve learned to wait. And on such an occasion as this it would be wrong if I did not remind you that we are reaping what others sowed. The men of noble faith and dauntless courage have passed away, but we who have entered into their labours will keep their memory green and fragrant. But we were not white-livered, and by plodding steadily along we have, by God's blessing, been enabled to perform a humble but necessary work. And now—would you believe it?—we ask for more opportunities of extended usefulness. I must not occupy your time unduly, for other speakers will develop our programme, but you have probably gathered what is our next aim. By the open-handed generosity of many friends we are in a position to make considerable additions to this building, and your committee are of opinion that this increased space will afford room for classes for the working girls, and maybe for a kind of club-house for them. Some of the speakers are to discuss the question of co-education, a clumsy word for what seems to be a sensible sort of schooling. But whether we are to adopt mixed classes, or whether the sexes shall be kept apart, will largely depend upon the results of your deliberations to-night. There is doubtless a lot to be said in favour of mixed classes, but, no doubt some consider them undesirable. The only point to which you are definitely committed is that it is the women and girls we are to provide for next; but apart from that you are free to advise as to the best and most expeditious method by which the desire of our hearts may be fulfilled. I call upon our kind and honoured friend, Dr. Alton Locke, to propose the first resolution, which the Lady Bountiful will second.

Among the numerous privileges of wealth may confidently be reckoned an earnest appeal—to which, to their credit be it said, the possessors of riches are rarely reluctant to respond —to preside.

At a Bazaar.

Ladies and Gentlemen,—When your secretary sounded me, as if I were the deep sea, upon the likelihood of my being at liberty to open this bazaar, I confess I was somewhat taken back. A well-known Eastern traveller once told me about the bazaars in Cairo, what delightful places they are, how quaint and full of interest, where your pockets are relieved of their spare cash, not by light-fingered gentry but by glib-tongued and persuasive merchants, before you quite realise what is going on. So I was disposed at first to be guarded in my answers. But he soon reassured me, informing me that I might leave my notes at home, so long as I brought my cheque-book with me. That seemed to him entirely satisfactory. I next reminded him that bazaars had been the subject of a good deal of adverse criticism; but he promptly replied that that need not deter me, adding that several Acts of Parliament dealing with Rating and other matters had also been criticised in a spirit that was not altogether friendly and had survived the ordeal. I felt there was some force in his argument, that at any rate perhaps I ought not to condemn what seemed to be a popular institution because of an abuse here and there. Accordingly, I undertook to judge of this bazaar on its merits, having been satisfied on my main objection that the articles should not be offered for sale at prices which undercut the shopkeepers in the neighbourhood. And now, with Marshal MacMahon, I may say, "*J'y suis, J'y reste.*" I mean to have a walk round by and by, when I hope I may be followed by a large train of influential and well-to-do people, who have only recently discovered many wants, which shall be supplied at one or other of the beautiful stalls I see around me. I think none of us is under any delusion as to the object with which bazaars are held. They are believed to be an easy way of raising the wind, a figure of speech which explains why we are so anxious to come down with the dust. It is a strange thing that people will part much more readily with kind than with cash. I hope I am betraying no secrets when I say that what I have heard from lady friends leads me to infer that it would be cheaper if they induced their husbands to send a cheque at once and save the money spent upon materials and the time utilised in the working of them up into cosies and cakes. That is probably a mere man's point of view, for one lady triumphantly retorted "But, then, it's so *nice* to work for the Church!" [*Or Chapel, or whatever the object may be.*] But however that may be, Ladies and Gentlemen, it is a most excellent thing to get rid of debt. Debt is an unmitigated curse. It hangs like a millstone around the neck of its slave, whether church, or chapel, or club, or person. I will not go so far as to adopt and adapt the old saying, "Get out of debt, honestly, if you can, but get out of debt." But I hope your efforts here may end in freedom. So, Ladies and Gentlemen, I declare the bazaar open. Now, let me, like Simple Simon, taste your wares!

Charity has claims which no chairman, *in posse* or *in esse* can resist. With perfect propriety, therefore, we may place him in the chair

At a Hospital Meeting

Ladies and Gentlemen.—To-day we meet on common ground where we are remote from strife and tumult, for we are assembled to consider what can be done to enhance the usefulness of our Hospital and Dispensary. The distractions of the political world have no concern for us, and combatants on all sides will rejoice to take off their armour and put aside their weapons of war, to unite in a combined effort on behalf of the suffering and sick poor. Even as we contemplate the beneficent work before us, we already seem to breathe "an ampler ether, a diviner air," George Gilfillan once wrote that sympathy was better than speech, when regretting his inability to attend a meeting. And, Ladies and Gentlemen, sympathy counts for much, but it is neither the beginning nor the end. We must, in fact, be careful that it does not carry us away. We should present a sorry spectacle if we allowed our sympathy to evaporate in smoke. We are all aware of the truly admirable work which the Hospital is constantly doing, and it would be lamentable were its staff of self-sacrificing and devoted doctors, surgeons, and nurses crippled in their noble efforts merely for want of the increased accommodation admitted to be urgently needed.

.   .   .   .   .

[Here speak with feeling about the particular work the hospital is doing.]

In the face of these facts I do not envy the man who is obliged to turn away a case from the doors with the words "No room; every bed full." It recalls the awful despair in Dante's terrible line, which I venture slightly to modify to suit the situation, "All hope abandon; ye cannot enter here." Do I express our feelings too forcibly, Ladies and Gentlemen, when I say that such a calamity must be averted at all costs? It is unnecessary to labour the critical position that confronts us, for we are within measurable distance of that dread day. The time for action has arrived, and I hope that the speeches we are to listen to now will abound with practical suggestions. Briefly, the two chief points which we have to discuss are more wards and more money. They are, of course, intimately related, but can be kept separate in our deliberations. What I mean is that we shall be addressed by some of our medical experts on the one subject, and by some business specialists on the other, who will tell us how we may best organise ourselves with a view to collecting the largest possible sum of money in the shortest possible time. Money! Money! Money! The want of it hampers the noblest works of society. They call it the "sinews of war": far more truthfully it is the sinews of peace. And now, I think, we may proceed to business. The order of debate which I propose to lay down is this: in the first place, we shall learn exactly what accommodation is needed to keep the Hospital and Dispensary abreast of the requirements of the times; and, in the second, having ascertained this and the probable cost of it, we shall be able to deal effectively with the readiest means of procuring adequate financial support. Our first group of speakers will confine themselves to the first topic, our second to the second. That will simplify discussion and help us to turn our meeting to the best possible account. When we come to the second point, I urge that it may be regarded in the spirit of the Apostle's dictum:—"And now abideth faith, hope, love, those three; but the greatest of these is love." Dr. Goodenough will move the first resolution, Nurse Deering will second it, and various members of the hospital staff will speak to it.

Dr. Goodenough!

In northern climes especially, winter, like youth, is the season of improvement. It is the time when the lecture is still one of the leading features of social life. This form of entertainment needs a chairman to "round it off," to give an aspect of completeness to the function. We may, therefore, finish these speciments of typical speeches by listening to the chairman.

At a Popular Lecture.

Ladies and Gentlemen.—I was reading the other day a story told by the Marquis of Tullibardine about a Highland grand dame who engaged a crofter's son as a page. The lad was, of course, provided with a suit of livery adorned with buttons. One evening a dinner-party was to be held, and, as the hour drew near, the boy put his shock head into the lady's boudoir and said, "Please, ma'am, am I to wear my ain breeks or yours?" Well, that uncertainty need not arise here. You have not met to listen to me, but to our friend on my right, who will, I am sure, amply reward you for the trouble you have taken to attend in spite of the inclement weather. [*Should the evening be delightful, the remark will run otherwise—"in spite of the attractions elsewhere."*] Nevertheless, I crave your indulgence while I address you for a few minutes in my "ain breeks." There was a time, as some of you will remember, when lectures were in universal request. Most churches, chapels, and institutions ran a course, and it was not always easy to keep pace with the demand. But the lecture still holds its own, although it has formidable rivals in the cinema, the dance hall, and the bridge club. I am certain, however, that, so long as we have men [*or women*] like our friend to entertain us, the lecture will remain a standing dish at the feast of reason and the flow of soul. Ladies and Gentlemen, I ask Mr. —— to favour us with his lecture on ——.

Thanks and Evermore Thanks.—Of course, the chairman's functions do not terminate with the delivery of an opening speech on the lines suggested in the examples just given. Consequently he must remain alert and vigilant, because in some cases he will have to propose a vote of thanks at the close. This duty, however, is better delegated to someone else either on the platform or in the "body of the meeting," whom he will call upon by name. (It is fair, though, to send notice of this intention by the secretary or other official, as few persons like to be asked to speak unprepared.) When the chairman undertakes it himself, his best plan is to be brief and cordial. Everybody is anxious to leave, and it is awkward when a visitor or entertainer who is publicly thanked has to express his acknowledgments in the turmoil caused by people putting on their overcoats, and perhaps engaging in conversation *sotto voce*. And the chairman himself must be thanked. Too frequently this is done in a disagreeably perfunctory manner. A voice is heard from the platform crying, "Vote of thanks to the chair!" and then the curtain is rung down. In point of fact, the post of chairman is by no means a sinecure. It may be onerous and responsible, and a great deal of anxiety may go with the conscientious performance of all its duties. He ought, therefore, to be formally thanked, the vote being proposed and seconded in due style, and put to the meeting by the mover of it, who must be careful to call for the "against" votes, as well as for the *pros*, if only to have the gratifying assurance to tender to the chairman that he had been thanked "unanimously and with acclamation." The whole of the little ceremony need not last more than two or three minutes, but it should never be neglected, and every attempt should be made by the promoters of a meeting to keep the house until the chairman has uttered his modest, "Thank you very much, Ladies and Gentlemen."

THE SECRETARY'S COMPANION

CHAPTER XVI

THE COMPANY SECRETARY : MEETINGS.

Secretary's Duties.—The duties of a secretary in connection with meetings of shareholders begin earlier than do those of the chairman. He must see that every shareholder without exception receives notice. This he must do whether the meeting is ordinary or extraordinary.

Section 112 of the Companies Act, 1929 says:—

"A general meeting of every company shall be held once at the least in every calendar year and not more than fifteen months after the holding of the last preceding general meeting."

The above-mentioned general meetings are called ordinary general meetings; other general meetings are called extraordinary general meetings.

To guard against any member's being unnotified, there should be a double check, the first made by some one calling over the members' register while the secretary sees that there is a notice and admission card corresponding to each name, and the second by the assistant calling through the addressed envelopes (into which the admission cards and notices have now been put) while the secretary lightly pencil ticks in the register as each name is called. The totals should then be agreed, and an entry made and confirmed by signatures of the number of notices and the time and place of posting.

Wording of Extraordinary Notice.—In summoning an extraordinary general meeting the secretary must be careful that his wording is sufficiently elastic. On page 37 we

saw that the chairman's hands are tied as regards the amendments he may accept—that, for example, if the meeting were
summoned to sanction an increase of the company's capital
by £30,000, an amendment to increase this to £60,000 would
be *ultra vires*. The discussion might show that the smaller
amount was thought insufficient by the majority, who would
vote down the motion unless amended. This being legally
impossible, another extraordinary meeting is necessary. All
this trouble would have been saved had the notice been less
precise. Instead of "to increase the capital of the company
by £30,000," the notice might have run "by whatever amount
shall be deemed necessary to carry out such and such improve-
ments" or "by £30,000 or whatever amount, etc." But if
the directors are opposed to any alteration of the sum, and
would, indeed, rather abandon the whole project than be
overruled on this point, the notice cannot be too precise.
It will be seen that the wording of the notice of an extraordinary general meeting demands the secretary's very close
attention.

Agenda and Agenda Book.—When drafting notices of an
ordinary general meeting, which will include a summary of
the business to be discussed, is a convenient time for drawing
up the agenda, a copy of which should be in the chairman's
hands some days before the meeting. Now, too, is a good
time for making the left-hand column entry in the Agenda
Book.

The Agenda Book may be described as a minute book in
two columns, in the first of which the secretary enters the
matters to be settled at the meeting, beginning with the
minutes of the last meeting, and following this with the other
points in the order in which he has decided that they shall
be taken.

In preparation for the meeting he writes up the left-hand
column. In the right he will record the decisions arrived
at as they are made. We give an example of the book at
the completion of the meeting.

Agenda.   Fourth Ordinary General Meeting — June,
                   ——, of the —— Company, Limited.

Minutes last meeting.	Read, confirmed, signed.
Report and Accounts.	Adopted.

Dividend.	Proposed by chair and seconded by Mr. —— that dividend of — % be distributed. Carried *Nem. Con.*
Resignation of Sir Arthur H——	Proposed by Dr. B. and seconded by Canon C. that Sir Arthur H. be asked to continue on the Board. Carried *Nem. Con.* Sir A. consents.
and so on.	

After this the secretary will probably refresh his memory by a careful scrutiny of the minutes of the last meeting, which it will be one of his first duties at the coming meeting to read.

The Minutes and Their Values.—The general meeting minutes record all proceedings and resolutions of the company's general meetings, whether ordinary or extraordinary. It is of the first importance that they should be kept correctly, without omissions of anything material. In the event of legal proceedings arising, the Minute Book can become decisive evidence. Of itself, however, it is not always nor necessarily decisive. For example, the fact that a resolution alleged to have been passed is not recorded in the Minute Book is not complete proof that it was not. An unrecorded resolution can be proved by verbal evidence, but this must be very clear and strong.

The usual form of minutes is known, but for the benefit of those who have never acted as secretary, we append a form upon which they can model them. The writing should be clear, and sufficiently spaced out to admit of possible alterations, which should be initialled when made, in order to verify the corrections. It is well to leave a margin on one side.

The Form of the Minutes.—"Minutes of the Third Ordinary Meeting of the —— Company, Limited, held on the 10th June, 19— at (the registered office of the Company) at — o'clock.

"*Present*:—(Here insert the chairman first.)
"John Smith, Esq., in the chair.

"Messrs. So-and-So, and So-and-So—(in order).

"The notice calling the meeting was read by the secretary.

"The Minutes of the General Meeting held on of   , were then read by the secretary, confirmed by the meeting, and signed by the chairman.

"The Report of the Directors, and the statement of the Accounts of the Company were unanimously agreed to, on the motion of Mr. ——, seconded by Mr. ——.

[If the report, etc., be agreed to be taken as read by the meeting, this item of the proceedings should be first recorded in the minutes.]

"Upon the motion of the chairman, seconded by Mr. ——, it was unanimously resolved that a dividend of, etc.

"Upon the motion of Colonel ——, seconded by Mr. ——, it was unanimously resolved that Mr. —— be, and he is hereby declared, elected a director of the company in place of Mr. ——, who has resigned."

It is customary to pass a vote of thanks to the chairman before closing the business, and this, too, will be recorded. It is not actually necessary, but is sometimes done, to add a note of the time the meeting has lasted, thus:—"Duration of meeting, 1 hour 15 minutes."

If an amendment is moved after the seconding of any motion, it will appear on the minutes somewhat as follows:—

"It was moved by ——, and seconded by ——, that the Report and Accounts be adopted.

"Thereupon an amendment was moved by Mr. ——, and seconded by Mr. ——, that—[then appears the amendment from the terms of the paper handed to the chairman]. "This amendment, moved by ——, seconded by ——, was put to the meeting by the chairman, and negatived.

"The original proposition was then put and carried, the numbers being —— for and —— against."

The various motions and resolutions should be entered in the following form:—

"It was moved by ——, seconded by ——, and resolved, that"—(here follow the terms of the resolution). If the resolution has passed without any dissentient voice, the word "unanimously," or the Latin phrase *nemine contradicente*

I

(*nem. con.*), may be inserted. The latter is preferable. "Unanimously" states that everyone approved. Some member may have disapproved silently, and may subsequently protest against the recorded unanimity. *Nem. con.* states a fact.

When a report or balance sheet is passed and adopted, it is usual to paste in, or otherwise insert, a copy of the document in the Minute Book, so that the papers referred to may be in evidence. In point of fact, it is a wise precaution for the secretary to insert, at its proper place in the book, every document of importance, so that the minutes may form a complete and authentic record of the salient transactions at the meeting.

The usual resolution of a vote of thanks to the chairman may be signed by the proposer of it in the Minute Book; but this is omitted more often than not.

The foregoing is the general and most easily acquired form. The minutes are compiled from rough notes, or from shorthand taken at the time, care being exercised in the transcription of the copies of the resolutions and amendments, which the chairman handed to the secretary when he received them from the mover.

Exclusion of Strangers.—Clerks (one is not enough) should be told off to be at the door to see that no unqualified persons gain admission. The doorkeepers should be furnished with a list of members so that they may tick each name as the shareholder hands in his *signed* ticket. Sometimes entrants are asked to sign the register.

Messenger at Hand.—The secretary should appoint someone to be at his beck and call while the meeting is in progress, otherwise he may find himself called away to answer the telephone while vital business is under discussion, or have his attention distracted by some trumpery matter that a junior could have settled. The secretary must be there all the time and "all there" all the time.

Secretary and Chairman.—The secretary, who usually sits beside the chairman so as to keep him posted, will make his tuition as inconspicuous as possible, because it detracts from the chair's authority to speak obviously under instruction. For this reason the wise secretary gets the schooling done before the meeting. Knowing the course the business will be likely to take, he anticipates the problems that will confront his chief and supplies him with anticipatory solutions.

The Secretary Intervenes.—The secretary never intervenes publicly except at the request of the chair. Called upon to speak, he does so as briefly and dryly as possible, confining himself to statement of fact. For example, a proposal has been made that the chairman believes to be *ultra vires.* He appeals to the secretary. The secretary reads the article governing the question, and sits down. If the article forbids the course that has been suggested it is not necessary for the paid official to say so. The meeting will take the point, or if it does not the chairman will push it home. The secretary keeps outside controversy.

Procedure at General Meetings.—This will be found fully described in the first part of this volume. The information in the chapters entitled "Company Meetings," "Polls and Proxies," "Motions and Amendments" is as valuable to secretary as to chairman. Indeed what is there that a chairman should know that a secretary can neglect? If there is a difference, it is that the secretary's mastery of the facts must be more complete; for whereas the chair has some one to consult, the secretary must answer unprompted or admit incompetence.

Directors' Meetings.—In sending out notices of a directors' meeting the secretary will see to it that the accompanying agenda lists end thus—"Other business if any." He cannot foresee everything. At the meeting some question he has not thought of will be raised, and if there is no agenda heading that covers it, the discussion may be stopped, or, if allowed to continue, made the ground of complaint subsequently by an absentee. "If I had thought that So-and-So were coming up I should have made a point of attending. But the agenda list's silence on this, combined with its mention of less important matters, distinctly implied that it would not be discussed. I should certainly have been told." And the poor secretary is in hot water.

Pass Book, etc.—The secretary will take with him to the meeting the Pass Book, which has just been written up, the Cash Book and a statement he has prepared reconciling their respective totals, showing the paid cheques that have not yet been presented and any received cheques not yet credited. Among his papers, too, will be a statement of all the share-transfers that have been made since the last meeting of the board.

Sometimes it is necessary to prepare statistics showing the comparative business done by the company during the last month and in the corresponding month last year. If he has not had time to post a copy of this to the chairman, he must take the opportunity to give it to him before the meeting begins so that the chairman may himself make the statement should he wish. The last thing a judicious secretary wishes is to appear wiser or better informed than his chief.

During the Meeting.—As soon as a quorum has assembled it is the secretary's duty to direct the chairman's attention to the fact. The meeting then proceeds to the business on the agenda. The secretary, who better than anyone else knows how essential it is that certain things should be settled that afternoon, will adroitly keep the chairman (and the board too, if need be) up to time. As each new topic arises he will be ready for it, with any documents relating to it in his hands, duly docketed and in the order in which they will be required.

Short of actual incompetence, nothing so gives away a secretary as his fumbling among a mass of ill-assorted papers, or diving into this or that pocket for a letter of first-rate importance, perhaps at the end of this delay having to make the humiliating confession that he "must have left the letter at home."

Before the Directors Disperse.—Before the meeting breaks up the secretary will see that all cheques and documents he has brought with him for signature have been signed properly, and that all decisions are expressed in writing by the chairman, particularly if these involve secretarial action. Verbal instructions are *not* enough, inaccuracy both in expression and in apprehension being all too easy. Every director, before he goes, must sign the Directors' Attendance Book.

Writing Up the Minutes.—This should be done the same day, while recollection is still vivid, even if it is believed that nothing has been left to memory. Out of the many points settled there may be one on which the written word itself may, after a lapse of time, become ambiguous when all memory of the attendant circumstances has faded. There is this further advantage in writing up the various decisions promptly, that this may remind the secretary of some immediate duty whose execution, otherwise, might have been delayed.

Separate Minute Book.—Some secretaries keep the minutes of board meetings at the end of the General Meeting Minute Book. This is not advisable. A shareholder has the right to see the General Meeting Minutes. It is not seemly that he should have access to a volume containing a record of what the directors have decided among themselves. Let there be a separate record, therefore, for the deliberations of the board.

The Companies Act, 1929, Sec. 121 establishes the right of members to inspect the General Meeting Minute Book.

"The books containing the minutes of proceedings of any general meeting of a company held after the commencement of this Act shall be kept at the registered office of the company, and shall, during business hours (subject to such reasonable restrictions as the company may by its articles or in general meeting impose, so that not less than two hours in each day be allowed for inspection) be open to the inspection of any member without charge."

Members must be supplied, if they demand this, with copies of any such minutes at a charge of sixpence or less per hundred words.

CHAPTER XVII

MINISTERIAL AND CLERICAL.

Secretary a Servant.—The duties of a company secretary are clerical and ministerial. Unlike the honorary secretary or the secretary (paid or unpaid) of a charity, who is expected to be its dynamic force, the company secretary does not direct or initiate its operations. Its success or failure does not depend upon him, although good work in his department, as in every other, makes for the success of the whole. He does not make contracts, although he may draw up the agreements that arise from them, and his control is limited to the office, and possibly to but a part of that, the accountant's department being sometimes independent. Travellers, salesmen and agents do not look to him for direction, but to general and departmental managers, all of whom, like the secretary himself, being under the authority of the directors. It is roughly true to say that the board of directors is the employer and the secretary their servant. Consequently the secretary's word does not bind the company unless those dealing with the concern have been given some special reason, by past transactions, etc., for believing that the secretary has more power in his hands than his nominal position gives him. In this he is in exactly the same position as a clerk in a private business. Because the secretary's promise does not bind his company, it does not follow that it will have no effect. It may have results disastrous to himself. There may be grounds for action against him. A secretary, therefore, should make no promises, except on express instructions from the board—from the board, mark, not from a single director, however dominant.

But although a secretary is merely a servant in such matters as business undertakings, he has direct personal responsibility for the rendering of statutory returns to the registrar. The penalty for omission falls upon the secretary himself. He must not take orders, even from the board, that contravene the statutes; if he does he cannot shelter behind directorial instructions. These, however explicit and peremptory, will not exonerate him.

Duties.—The duties of a secretary are:—

1. Business connected with general and directors' meetings. (These were considered in our last chapter.)
2. Keeping of registers, and making statutory returns, etc.
3. Correspondence.
4. Preparation of agreements.
5. Control of cash and banking accounts.
6. Signing of cheques and bills.
7. Office control.

The Registers.—The keeping of the registers below-mentioned is compulsory, and all must be retained at the registered office of the company. Some, everyone has the right to inspect; others, only the shareholders can see of right; but whatever the regulations, they must be observed, or heavy penalties are incurred.

Register of Members.—This records the name, address, and occupation of every member, usually across the top of the page devoted to him, thus:—

Samuel   Pickwick   Gentleman
    34 Goswell Road, London, E.C. (Retired Sugar Broker)

Below this is a ruling in columns, like that of a one-page ledger, the columns on the credit side recording the date of membership, distinctive numbers of shares bought, amount paid; the debtor side showing date of cessation of membership, and particulars of shares transferred.

Index.—The Companies Act, 1929, Section 96 says:—

"Every company having more than fifty members shall, unless the register of members is in such a form as to constitute in itself an index, keep an index of the names of the members of the company and shall, within fourteen days after the date on which any alteration is made in the register of members, make any necessary alteration in the index."

Where there are numerous shareholders, necessitating a many-volumed register, the loose-leaf system is the best, with an index for each letter. The accounts are kept in alphabetical order and numbered, there never being more than one account on a page, an account requiring several pages retaining the same number throughout.

Annual Summary.—Every year on the fourteenth day after the general meeting a list embodying these particulars must be made, and a summary showing capital, number of shares, number of shares taken, calls per share, total received from calls, total unpaid, total of shares forfeited, names and particulars of shares held by persons who have ceased to be members since the last list was prepared, etc. This summary must be entered in a different part of the register from that showing each member's individual holding, and must be completed within twenty-eight days after the meeting. A copy must forthwith be sent to the registrar of Joint Stock Companies.

Right of Access to Register of Members.—Anybody has the right to inspect this register; shareholders gratis, others on the payment of one shilling or less. (The company's regulations may reduce this charge, but cannot increase it.) Anyone can demand a copy to be made of any part of it at a charge of sixpence per hundred words, but no one may himself make a copy. Actually "a period of ten days commencing on the day next after the day on which the requirement is received by the company." It must be available for inspection at least two hours every working day, except for thirty days in the year, when it may be closed for the preparation of the dividend. The right to inspect the register includes the right to see and use the index. (Companies Act, 1929, Sec. 98.)

Outsiders having these rights, the secretary must not show surliness in granting facilities incidental to them. On the other hand he should not actively assist in any search, for thereby he might be making himself a party to some procedure hostile to a member, or even to the company itself.

Politeness that stops short of effusiveness and a cheerful rendering of what cannot be denied are sufficient. Even if the secretary knows that the object of the inspection is some injury to the company, he must not forbid it.

Register of Mortgages.—All that the Act requires is that this should record a description of the property mortgaged, the amount of the mortgage, and the names of the mortgagees. It is customary, however, to make the record somewhat more detailed, in order that it may be of some practical value.

The regulations as to inspection, etc., are the same as those concerning the register of members, except that creditors, equally with shareholders, have the right of free inspection of the register and the copies of instruments creating the charge, and the company is not bound to supply copies. The register is to open "at all reasonable times," and those who inspect may make extracts.

Register of Debenture Holders.—Shareholders and registered holders of debentures have the right to inspect this, free. No one else has any right of inspection. The company is bound to supply copies at the rate of sixpence per hundred words, and the register is open for inspection for the same periods as the register of members.

These three registers, namely of members, of mortgages and of debenture holders, are the only ones that persons, beyond the directors and auditors, have any legal right to inspect. No one may deny anything to an Inspector of the Board of Trade.

Inspection by Board of Trade.—The holders of one-tenth of the capital have the right to petition the Board of Trade to make an examination into the affairs of the company. If the petition is granted, the inspector to whom the enquiry has been deputed must be shown and told everything he wishes to see and hear. He has even the power to examine the secretary upon oath.

Register of Directors.—Changes in the directorate must be entered as they occur, and notice posted within fourteen days to the registrar, to whom also must be sent (included in the annual return) a list of the names and addresses of persons who at the date of the return are directors of the company, or occupy the position of directors, by whatever name called.

Where one company controls another that company is the "person" who occupies the position of director, and should figure in the list, not the directors of the controlling company. Secretaries are sometimes uncertain about this.

Register of Transfers.—It is from the transfer register that entries for the register of members are obtained. The care demanded in dealing with transfers justifies the adjective so often misused "meticulous". The points upon which the secretary when handling transfers will be "careful with fear" are:—

a. The production of a proper instrument of transfer, correctly stamped.

b. The initialling of alterations (if any) by all parties to the transfer.

c. Verification of transferor's signature by comparison with his signature appearing on the transfer deed by which he acquired the shares.

d. The recording, on being advised of a shareholder's death or on seeing report of it in a newspaper, of the fact against his name in the register, to prevent the sending out of any dividend or the making of any transfer until probate and letters of administration have been produced.

e. The sending of a notice, before a transfer is made, to the registered holder that this is about to be done, in order that he may intervene if any fraud is being attempted.

f. The production and cancellation of the transferor's share certificate.

Lost Papers.—If the loss of share certificates is reported by the lawful holder, the secretary will make an entry to that effect in the register, and thus prevent any fraudulent transfer; but he will not issue new documents for many months, and even then will demand a letter of indemnity. Dividends, however, will be paid in the meantime as before. Somewhat similarly he will treat inability to produce some of the documents necessary to the completion of the purchase of a new issue—the letter of allotment or the receipts for instalments paid—demanding a letter of indemnity and insisting on a considerable period of delay.

Allotment Letters.—There must be no possibility of omissions in the despatch of these. A method that has been found to work well is for the secretary to have the allotment letters bound in a book with counterfoils upon which can be entered particulars of their despatch. Any steps that can be taken beforehand to facilitate dispatch are desirable, for delay is only less dangerous than error. Until the letter of allotment has been posted the application for shares upon which it is based may be withdrawn.

Within a month of a company's making an allotment full details concerning it must be filed with the registrar.

Notice must be sent to the registrar of any increase of share capital within fifteen days of the passing of the resolution authorizing it.

Auditors.—Auditors have right of access at all times to all books, accounts and vouchers, and the secretary should meet any demands of this nature cheerfully. Nor should he resent it if asked to furnish proof as regards his own payments or receipts; for it is one of the maxims of accountancy that no servant's uncorroborated statement on such a point should be accepted. At the same time it is not the duty of an accountant to go to work as if he were opening a criminal investigation, and if by such a misconception of his duties he is upsetting the staff, a tactful word from the secretary may do good. It was wittily said by Lord Justice Lopes in the Kingston Cotton Mill Case: "An auditor is not bound to be a detective, to approach his work with suspicion, or with a foregone conclusion that there is something wrong. He is a watchdog, not a bloodhound."

Requirements of Companies Act, 1929.—"Section 122 of the Act declares:—

"1. Every company shall cause to be kept proper books of account with respect to—

"*a.* All sums of money received and expended by the company and the matters in respect of which the receipt and expenditure takes place.

"*b.* All sales and purchases by the company.
"*c.* The assets and liabilities of the company.

"2. The books of the company shall be kept at the registered office of the company or at such other place as the directors may think fit, and shall at all times be open to inspection by the directors."

Correspondence.—Letters should be written in English and not in the jargon of the counting-house, and tersely; but if the meaning cannot be conveyed adequately in a few words, more must be employed. Neither the allure of alliteration nor the temptation to give a neat turn to a sentence should be allowed to deflect the writer by a hair's breadth from what he has set out to say. Eloquence and humour are out of place in business communications. If tempted to either, let the secretary imagine himself hearing the contemplated purple passage read aloud at a board meeting.

Writing to a shareholder the secretary must not lose his sweetness and light even when replying to some ridiculous complaint, for this will have proceeded from stupidity, which is an affliction rather than a fault. Whatever the provocation, sarcasm is never permissible.

While on the subject of correspondence with shareholders, it may be as well to remind secretaries that any member has a right to demand a copy of the memorandum of association and the articles (if any) on payment of one shilling.

"Any member of a company whether he is or is not entitled to have sent to him copies of the company's balance sheets and any holder of debentures of a company shall be entitled to be furnished, on demand, without charge, with a copy of the last balance sheet of the company, together with a copy of the Auditor's report on the balance sheet." Companies Act, 1929, Sec. 130.

Preparation of Agreement, &c.—This the secretary will see to in connection with the company solicitor. In the very rare event of there being any serious difference of opinion between them on a vital matter the secretary must not lightly give way. It is true that probably he would be exonerated for any step taken on the solicitor's instructions;

but if he is worth his salt, the secretary's first concern is not his own immunity from censure, but the company's welfare.

The secretary's unescapable responsibilities are many and varied. He must see that the documents he handles are sufficiently stamped, and that when adhesive stamps are permissible, these have been properly cancelled by the person who is responsible for this by the writing across them of his initials or those of his firm or company and the true date of his writing them.

When any proxies are sent in, it is incumbent upon the secretary to see that they are stamped properly, that they have arrived in time to permit of their remaining at the registered office of the company for the requisite qualifying period for their use at the coming meeting, and that the signers and holders alike are qualified to act.

Office Control.—Much, both as regards efficiency and economy, will depend upon the secretary's attitude towards his staff. If he is helpful towards their advancement and not grudging, the office will be run well and as cheaply as it ought to be. Perhaps as cheaply as it *can* be; for the Americans have taught us that high pay to the worker results often in a low cost per unit of work done. Cheap service, almost invariably, is bad service. A clerk won't give his best for your worst, and you, lacking will to reward and ability to punish, can't make him; for you fear the loss of one whom you believe you are defrauding more than he dreads dismissal from a bad job.

Modern office accessories, addressographs, calculating machines, and improved filing systems, soon repay their initial cost, but they are not fool-proof, and it is a mistake to think that anyone can be trusted to run them. The combination of an improved system with an unimproved junior is often disastrous. Don't we know the office whose handsome filing cabinet is the grave of documents consigned to it? Never again can they be brought to light. The fact is that much of the work we are accustomed to think entirely mechanical requires a closeness of attention that comes only by training. Know for certain that your assistant can give this skilled care before entrusting him with the bestowal of papers that must be accessible to you quickly.

Punctuality should be insisted upon, not only because it secures a fair day's work, but also because it helps to develop efficiency all round. The secretary will be best served who is particular but not pettifogging, and more apt to stimulate by example and encouragement than to depress by scolding and threats. As far as possible he should contrive that everyone does *some* work that is educative.

Discretion.—Much may hang upon a secretary's reticence. His is a position of trust. Nothing that passes in the office or the board room must be told outside. This, of course, can be said of almost any business situation, but secretaries are confronted by a difficulty more or less unique in having to resist their own shareholders. Is it certain that they should be held at arm's length? They own the whole concern; why must its inner workings be kept secret from them? The answer is that any verbal confidences must of necessity be partial in their effect. It would be manifestly unjust, for example, that country shareholders should be anticipated by London in respect to items of good or bad news. On the strength of some secretarial tip London members might buy shares that the more distant in ignorance were selling, or by their free buying might so raise the price of the stock that by the time the distant shareholders heard the good news its market value had been already lost. The opposite would occur if it were a tip to sell. The country shareholders would have no opportunity of selling except at the depreciated price. As regards company confidences, shareholders are treated as the outside public until properly advised simultaneously. Till there's news for all, there's news for none.

Similar considerations forbid secretaries and directors from speculating in their own company's shares. It isn't *fair* that they should skin the cream off the market. We have read of companies whose rule it is that after the board have fixed the coming dividend, directors are not allowed to disperse until a messenger has conveyed their decision to the secretary of the London Stock Exchange.

CHAPTER XVIII

SECRETARY OF COMPANIES.

So far we have been considering the secretary as employed by a single company needing all the service that he and a staff of assistants can render it. But there are companies of a humbler sort that cannot afford a secretary apiece, nor have they sufficient secretarial work to keep him employed. So they farm it out to some one who specialises on meeting precisely this need and who, for an agreed annual sum, will not only do all necessary work, but in addition provide an office that will serve as the registered address of the company (as required by the Act) and a place for the holding of all its meetings, board and general.

Providing a Place of Meeting.—The secretary's commitments under this head seem very formidable, but, as a matter of fact the accommodation provided is usually quite unpretentious, just a small outer office and an inner room containing a long table round which a dozen directors can sit. For general meetings there are small halls in the city of London that can be hired, but this is seldom necessary, the proportion of shareholders who attend general meetings being incredibly small. We knew a young and optimistic secretary of companies who, having sent out to two hundred shareholders notices of an extraordinary general meeting to consider a quite vital proposal, hired a hall for their accommodation. The directors came—and one shareholder. The canny secretary will postpone hiring until the overflowing general meeting materialises, having ascertained that the adjacent small hall he has in mind will be available if wanted. Usually a room that will hold the directors comfortably will contain the general meeting under pressure.

Duties.—The duties of the secretary of companies arising from statutory requirements are not less than those of the company secretary, the smallness of the concerns he serves not releasing him from any responsibilities under the Companies Act. Everything, therefore, in our last chapter is relevant to him, and he will probably, in addition, have to deal, at some time or other, with the starting and the winding up of companies. This we purposely deferred considering as being outside the purview of the average company secretary, who probably entered the corporation he serves as a junior and expects to leave it only as a pensioner.

Starting a Company.—If the secretary of companies is to hold his own, let alone make any progress, he must from time to time find new companies, for it is almost certain that some of his clients, sooner or later, will drop out. His opportunity will perhaps come from one of the directors with whom he has been working who is now contemplating the floating of a new company. As this at present has no legal existence, the form the appointment takes is to a secretaryship *pro tem.* with a personal promise that the position shall be made permanent in due course at so much a year. The temporary secretary will attend with his patron a number of meetings in which the details of the proposed company will be discussed and settled. A solicitor will be employed and he will take a leading part in preliminaries. The secretary-to-be will make the fullest use of the lawyer's expert knowledge now and subsequently. Every company has a solicitor and the secretary should not take any momentous step unadvised.

Of these discussions the temporary secretary will make full minutes and have them confirmed. These gatherings being somewhat informal, there is a temptation to omit the customary meeting routine, but the secretary, for his own protection, must see that it is observed.

Secretary as Trustee.—In the course of these preliminaries it may become necessary that certain properties should be acquired or undertakings made on behalf of the proposed company. As legally there is at present no company in existence there is no corporate body that can buy or promise. Some individual, therefore, must act as trustee, and it is not unusual for this responsibility to be thrust upon the temporary official. Whether he consents to accept it or not will depend upon his judgment of the conditions attending the particular case; but always he should, before involving himself, seek the advice of his own solicitor.

Registration of the Company.—Preliminaries having been arranged, the secretary is directed to obtain registration. This involves the lodging of certain documents with the Registrar of Companies. First in importance is—

The Memorandum of Association.—This being incomparably the most important document there will ever be drawn up in connection with the proposed company, it will have been framed by the promoters in consultation with a solicitor and perhaps counsel. "The Memorandum," says Lord Bowen, "contains the fundamental conditions on which alone the company is allowed to be incorporated." It must state:—

1. The name of the company with "Limited" as the last word of the name.
2. In what part of the United Kingdom the registered office is to be situated.
3. The objects of the company.
4. Statement that the liability of the members is limited.
5. The amount of the capital and how divided.

The Memorandum of Association of a public company must be signed by seven persons (two in the case of a private company) each of whom must state the particulars of the shares he is taking. (They are bound to take up and pay for the shares mentioned.) These signatures must be witnessed.

The Memorandum of Association need not be printed, but in the light of the fact that shareholders have the right to demand copies of it (see page 140) printing is advisable.

Statement of Capital.—This must be made out on form 25 and signed by a solicitor engaged in the flotation or someone mentioned in the articles as director or secretary. All the forms mentioned can be obtained from law stationers.

Declaration of Compliance.—(Form 41.) This, which declares that all the requirements of the Companies Act have been met, has the same regulations as to signature as the Statement of Capital.

K

List of Directors.—(Form 43.) This must be signed by the applicant. The inclusion on the "List of Persons who have Consented to be Directors" of the name of anyone who has *not* consented is a serious offence.

Articles of Association.—If the company means to have its own articles, these must be printed and registered with the Memorandum of Association. The new company, if a small concern, may be content to be ruled by Table A, or by Table A with certain qualifications, to suit its own particular circumstances. In the latter case, a brief document consisting of a statement that the regulations of Table A (full title) shall apply to the company, except articles Nos. So-and-so, and, under headings of subject (e.g.) "Voting" "Meetings," the Articles wanted in their stead.

On the strength of these documents, the necessary stamps having been affixed and the legal fees paid, the registrar will grant a Certificate of Incorporation.

"A Certificate of Incorporation given by the registrar in respect of any association shall be conclusive evidence that all the requirements of the act in respect of registration and of matters precedent and incidental thereto have been complied with." (Companies Act, 1929, Section 15.)

The Company in Existence.—Legally the new company has been in existence from the first minute of the day mentioned in the certificate. It can now act. The secretary should see to it that one of its first acts is to relieve him of any responsibilities as trustee that he may have incurred; and another to confirm the agreement provisionally made with him as to employment, salary, etc.

He, on his part, adds the name of the company to the others on his office door, hangs the Certificate of Incorporation, which he promptly has had framed, upon his walls, and starts the necessary registers. If the new company is quite a small concern, the secretary will do this speedily and easily. At a law stationer's it is possible to obtain all the statutory registers bound together to form different sections of one volume. A company having less than fifty members does not need to keep an index of the names of members. (Companies Act, 1929, Sec. 96.)

Notice of Registered Office.—The company now has its registered office to which all communications and notices must be addressed. A writ may be legally served on the company by leaving it at or by sending it by post to this address.

Notice of the situation of the registered office (and of any subsequent change therein) must be given to the registrar. Before the passing of the Act of 1929, notice could be filed any time before the start of business and there was no time prescribed for notification of change.

Getting New Business.—In the preceding pages we have shown a company, as it were, seeking a secretary. Too often, it is the secretary who must seek companies, and a hard search he finds it. His one ever-present anxiety is to replace with new concerns such of his companies as are failing in the struggle for existence, and the mortality rate among companies too small to employ secretarial staffs of their own is not low. Where, where is he to find this new blood? Solicitors and accountants have more patronage of this kind in their hands than most people. Sometimes accountants keep secretaryships of companies in their own hands—a sore point this with professional secretaries. In the discharge of his duty to the companies he serves, a secretary meets their auditors and legal advisers, and quite legitimately tries to impress them with his accuracy and diligence, nor can he be blamed for cultivating social relations with them and others of their professions whom he meets locally or in connection with his hobbies. Any business men of position may some day be concerned in the flotation of new companies. The wider a secretary's circle of acquaintances, therefore, the better. Not only must he *know*, but he must also *impress*. And how better can he impress his secretarial ability upon comparative strangers than by serving them, through some association they are interested in, as an unpaid secretary? Honorary secretaryships are of many kinds, political, social, sporting, charitable, etc. The sporting secretaryship is perhaps less valuable than the others as a business-getter. Running an Old Boys' football club that puts out, perhaps, six teams a week, involves much work; but while it introduces one to a fair number of men, it gives comparatively small opportunity for displaying business ability. Better for the purpose are political associations and charitable institutions. One shrinks from the association of philanthropy with self-seeking; but should the secretaryship of a charity be a-begging, with no one in sight willing, for disinterested reasons, to undertake the very onerous unpaid duties of the position, we see no harm in it being snapped up by an energetic, capable man who sees in it a possible stepping-stone to business advancement, provided that he sympathises with the society's objects and means to promote them by every means in his power.

The Chartered Institute of Secretaries.—Anyone who can get the appointments may become a secretary of companies, but it is a great aid to the acquisition of them to have the right to put the letters F.C.I.S. (Fellow of the Chartered Institute of Secretaries) or A.C.I.S. (Associate) after one's name, and the knowledge gained in the preparation for the very searching examinations involved will be of inestimable advantage in filling the positions when obtained. Fellows and Associates may describe themselves as Chartered Secretaries.

Transference of Company Secretaryships.—A secretary of companies will be well advised to keep in touch with others of the same calling. Occasionally a group of small companies will be losing its secretary, obliged by reason of age or infirmity to give them up, and his goodwill in them may be purchasable. On the basis of a payment to the retiring secretary of a percentage of the salaries actually received from these companies for a stated period of years, their acquisition may be advisable, as the augmented income will probably be unaccompanied by any increase of office expenditure. Of course, the retiring secretary cannot guarantee that all the companies can be transferred (the directors of some may have other views as to their disposal) but payments of percentage on salaries received meets the difficulty.

In many ways the position of a secretary of companies, combining as it does the salaried certainty of an employee (for a time at least) with the independence of a man in business for himself, is attractive. It would be ideal if company small fry were more permanent and the chance of their replacement less precarious.

CHAPTER XIX

THE HONORARY SECRETARY.

THE duties of an honorary secretary are by no means of a trivial character, and the society that is served by a capable and willing worker is very fortunate. The occupant of the post must be prepared to go through a good deal of what may be described as drudgery, and he will not receive a penny piece for his trouble until the day shall come when he retires. Then an illuminated address, or piece of plate, or gold watch, or it may even be a cheque—the fatter the better—will no doubt be presented to him, not as payment (for that is probably impossible) for his services, but in grateful acknowledgement of them.

Personal Endowments.—It goes without saying that a man of some education and tact should be selected for the post. The former is essential, because he is commonly entrusted with the correspondence, private and public, of the body for whom he is acting. As a rule, the bulk of his writing will be of a routine nature, mainly confined to entering up the minutes, giving effect to decisions, and letter-writing. Now and again, however, it does happen, in the case particularly of societies established for the discharge of business in which the public are interested, that he may be called upon to initiate or participate in correspondence in the Press. In such an event the secretary's letter would, if time allowed, be first submitted to his committee, whose acceptance or modification of its terms and expressions would relieve him of responsibility. But since it would be absurd, excepting in very rare circumstances, to convene a committee merely to consider the wording and argumentation of a letter, the secretary might have to contribute his quota to the correspondence columns of a daily newspaper, and be prepared to shoulder whatever criticism or blame it might provoke. As to tact, it is essential that the secretary should be able to manage men. Nearly every committee contains persons of peculiar temperament, sometimes even a faddist or crank, and the secretary must, therefore, be patient and occasionally appear to suffer fools gladly. He will get his work done most expeditiously—and this is the chief thing—by following the line of least resistance. Naturally, a committee chooses as its secretary a man of good address, for it may be necessary for him to do a certain amount of interviewing. In addition he must be well acquainted with the ordinary forms of business. However unworldly may be the object of the society for which he works voluntarily he must be a man of affairs with a sense of proportion, a practical idealist.

Summoning a Committee.—It may safely be assumed that the honorary secretary has to work with a committee. In the case of a society just formed, the first thing the secretary will have to do is to call the members to their opening meeting. Whether the summons will be by letter or postcard may be left to individual discretion. It may be doubted whether anyone in these days objects to receive postcards, but the secretary of course will never issue a summons for the discussion of private and confidential, or other important affairs, save in a sealed envelope. Some secretaries attend to the duty of summoning a committee rather casually, simply calling a meeting for such and such a date at such and such a time and place. But it is obviously over-sanguine to expect a number of men and women to assemble without having received a definite clue to the business to be transacted.

Minutes.—When the committee meeting assembles, the first thing to occupy it will be the reading of the minutes of the previous meeting. (Should it be a first meeting, there cannot be any minutes to offer, and in such case the secretary will recite the circumstances in which the committee came to be appointed, and read the full list as constituted.) He will next either send round the attendance-book for members to sign, or himself make a note of those present, the former being the better method, after which the agenda will be gone through systematically. We have dealt elsewhere (pp. 127–8) with this matter of the minute-book, and it will be unnecessary to repeat what has been said. Though it is the chairman's duty to take notes, in a book supplied to him for the purpose, of the business done and decisions arrived at, the secretary will keep his own notes for his own protection. He need not do this in an elaborate manner, since what is requisite is a record of the salient facts. Save when the matter is of moment and there is serious difference of opinion, he should not note the names of the various speakers and what they said. When decisions are unanimous, it will suffice to enter: "It was unanimously agreed to hold the annual dinner at the Blank Hotel on such a date," and so with other resolutions passed without dissent or virtually so.

After the Committee.—Discussion should be followed by action. As soon as the committee meeting has been recorded in the minutes, which is best done at once, the secretary should get to work to carry out the various tasks which have been imposed upon him. If the claims of his own business forbid an immediate start, he should begin as soon as ever he can. Procrastination is easy when a man's working hours are fully occupied with something else. But it must be conquered at least to the extent of getting the new departures well under way before the next committee assembles. Nothing will so discourage the members as to learn that between the two assemblies no progress has been made.

In reporting to the next committee meeting it will be well for the secretary not to go much into detail about what has yet to be accomplished. They have instructed him in general terms; it will be a loss all round if they are led to supplementing the general by the particular. Speaking broadly, a committee prefers to be confronted with accomplished facts.

As compared with his professional brother, the honorary secretary often appears slip-shod and untidy. This should not be. Neatness and method are more saving of time than their opposites and, after the initial effort, quite easily acquired. Let the honorary secretary, therefore, learn to take pride in his work. He will keep the minute-book in "apple-pie" order, entering each minute separately, and inserting in the broad, left-hand margin, which he will rule down every page the name of the topic dealt with in each paragraph. As minute-books and documents accumulate on his hands, let him provide house-room for them without complaint. If the society or institution of which he is the secretary is permanent, these things will ultimately form its archives, and be of no one can tell what interest to the next generation. If the secretary doesn't preserve them, he may rest assured that no one else can, since the presumption is that, owing to his carelessness, apathy, or neglect, they have been lost stolen, burnt, or dustbinned.

Should the Secretary Speak ?—As a rule, the secretary should not appear in too many rôles. In committee he cannot help having to talk often, answering questions, and tendering advice, since he holds all the ropes in his own hand. But in public, his duty should be limited to reading letters and making announcements, leaving to others the functions of oratory. He need not fear that he will be a mere figure-head, for he will have plenty to do in coaching others. When he has the requisite ability the secretary must always hold himself ready to fill a gap, or it may be to reply on the spot to an attack on his society or committee. Yet many most efficient secretaries lack the gift of public speech, a gift which is far from being indispensable to the adequate discharge of their office. These men, though not at home in fields of rhetoric, shine in the fulfilment of routine business; and, unable to speak, have skill to equip a chairman or other member of the institution with all the points, and possibly jokes, for a stop-gap speech, or with the facts and arguments for a crushing refutation of hostile criticism. Where there is time for preparation his coaching will be more thorough. In priming another person, the secretary should take the precaution, where possible, of preparing fairly full notes, in logical sequence, of the subjects to be publicly discussed, and be at hand to carry the speaker safely to the close of his oration. For similar practical reasons the secretary is in immediate attendance on his chairman at dinners of the society or committee with a view of posting him in such information as he may want, or even of enabling him to accomplish the customary duties at this social function without a hitch.

The Secretary-Treasurer.—As a rule, it is wisest to vest the duties of secretary and treasurer in separate persons.

In small societies, however, where the subscriptions are few, or little more than nominal, and donations from the public are neither solicited nor expected, or where the secretary is obliged to be in constant touch with the members, the posts are often combined, the secretary acting as treasurer and in that capacity receiving and acknowledging subscriptions. In the case of a tennis club, for example, it may be essential that the secretary should know whether members are or are not "clear on the books" before play in a match or tournament begins, and if he happens also to fill the post of treasurer he will be in a position to settle such a point definitely. The convenience of the joint-office is obvious in such circumstances. Whenever a secretary undertakes dual duty, however, he should make it an absolute rule invariably to present a financial statement at every committee meeting. Nevertheless, even when the secretary and treasurer are separate functionaries, the former frequently is required to act as his colleague's jackal. This sometimes arises from the fact that the treasurer, while perhaps of excellent business capacity, is notoriously inefficient in appealing for funds or for the payment of overdue subscriptions. Money being urgently needed, someone must be found to supplement the treasurer's feeble efforts, and who better than the secretary? Though such invidious duties do not fall within the scope of a secretary's operations, strictly regarded, yet where he is asked to discharge them to assist a brother-officer, he can hardly refuse to act.

The Secretary as Press Agent.—Publicity may not be so all-important as some people nowadays consider it, but it is important, and no secretary should omit recourse to it wherever he legitimately can. Of course it is essential that the affairs in which his committee are engaged should be of public interest, as this is the only plea to which an editor will give ear. The majority of secretaries, doubtless through ignorance or—dare it be said?—laziness, neglect to use the morning paper for the dissemination of news. Yet a clear and concise paragraph, sent to a news agency on the off-chance and duly circulated by that medium, may come to roost in more than one daily or weekly. Of course there are numerous occasions when the Press will be only too glad to send reporters, as in the case of public meetings. Then it will be incumbent on the secretary to issue these special tickets and to take care that adequate arrangements are made in the hall for their comfort. It may be that the object of the meeting is not deemed of sufficient importance for the Press to be directly represented; but the secretary need not despair on that account, for he may still communicate his own report to one of the Press agencies and use it as a channel of publicity. The advantage of dealing with an agency lies in the fact that it sends round all accepted matter to its clients, and the secretary's statement may thus be submitted to fifty or a hundred newspapers. The secretary needs hardly to be reminded that he must study brevity, write on one side of the paper only, and steer clear of everything libellous or provocative of litigation. When the function, though not itself public, really justifies and demands publicity, it will always be worth the secretary's while to call at a newspaper-office (giving it in this case what is called "exclusive" information) or agency to ascertain whether a reporter will attend or not. Should it be certain that one or more "pressmen" will be present, he must see to it that they are treated with due hospitality. If it is an open-air function—as a public "demonstration" or athletic or other similar gathering—which the secretary is managing, he must provide a Press tent (furnished with table and chairs), and ought also to arrange for two or three messengers to carry wires to the nearest telegraph station. To him every reporter will come for items of information and he must be duly posted in whatever subjects are likely to appeal to the inquiring journalistic mind. For this reason, too, the secretary must arrange to be personally in evidence for a considerable period, so that he may be at hand when "our own correspondent," or whatever other imposing designation the journalist may affect for the nonce, desires a few sentences of very special "copy". In fact, there is no end to the activities and enterprise for which the secretary must be prepared who seeks the publicity of the Press.

Parting Advice.—Every secretary sooner or later recognises the wisdom of certain homely proverbs or aphorisms, such as "If you want a thing done, do it yourself"; "Too many cooks spoil the broth"; and "It is the unexpected which happens". He must, therefore, be chary of delegating his duties to other than perfectly trustworthy persons. If, for instance, the Police must be notified of expected disturbance at a meeting he is organising, he should attend to this matter himself. It will not do to confess afterwards that he believed So-and-So was looking after it. He should not be too ready to discuss committee business with outsiders. What takes place in secret conclave may be gravely compromised by premature disclosure. He will, it seems scarcely necessary to say, be careful to keep copies of all letters of importance and not to mislay or destroy documents and papers. Nor will it do harm to cudgel his brains for new ideas or "happy thoughts" for the more adequate discharge of his duties. The secretary should not be too hidebound or conventional. Nothing succeeds like success, and departure from precedent may or may not be justified, but a spice of audacity may lead up to a fortunate *coup*. He never need fight shy of legitimate risks, and above all things, should he be saddled with great responsibility, he must, with due tact and discrimination, acquire a proportionate amount of power. A strong, honest, straightforward, amiable and truthful secretary is likely also to be, and cannot help being, masterful as well. And so good luck to him!

APPENDIX A

Brief Resumé of Points to be remembered.

THE CHAIR.

CHAIRMAN's authority should be absolute in meeting. When CHAIRMAN is speaking silence must be observed by others present.

When votes are equal on opposite sides the CHAIRMAN gives the casting vote.

When speaking is irregular, out of order, or irrelevant, the CHAIRMAN may interfere—and should do so. The CHAIRMAN may even stop irrelevant speech.

When meeting becomes noisy the CHAIRMAN may leave the chair, and adjourn the meeting; in such event no further business can be legally carried on.

The CHAIRMAN is always addressed by a member standing up.

The CHAIRMAN calls upon the first of two members who may rise. If the meeting call for the other, and the demand seem general, the CHAIRMAN may test the preference by a vote.

The decision of the CHAIRMAN should be obeyed.

MOTIONS.

All MOTIONS must be in writing, and in the affirmative form. They must be seconded.

[Purely formal motions are exempt from this rule, as regards being handed in in writing.]

No MOTION which has been already decided can be reproduced, whether in the same or other form, at the same meeting.

A MOTION may be withdrawn by the mover and seconder, provided the leave of the meeting has been obtained thereto.

AMENDMENTS.

All AMENDMENTS must be intelligible and relevant to the motion.

An AMENDMENT may be made to a suggested or proposed AMENDMENT, only in the event of the latter's being carried and put to the meeting as the original motion.

An AMENDMENT to *add words to a motion* can only be made by adding—not by deleting—words. For instance, if an amendment is proposed to a sentence which, it has been decided, "shall stand part" of a question, more words may be interpolated, but further words *cannot be omitted*.

If an AMENDMENT has been made to words in the middle of a motion, and someone seeks to amend the beginning of the same motion, the AMENDMENT to the amended one cannot be put until the way is cleared and the motion is restored to its original state by the withdrawal of the AMENDMENT proposed first.

Only one AMENDMENT should be proposed at a time.

An AMENDMENT may be withdrawn on the same terms as a motion. (*See* page 156.)

AMENDMENTS must be seconded, if the rules of the society or company so stipulate, but in the absence of such a rule an amendment need not be seconded (*See* page 62), and should, as a rule, be handed up in writing to the chair.

No AMENDMENT that is substantively the same as a former (decided) amendment may be put at the same meeting. (*See* Motions.)

SPEAKING.

SPEECHES must be clear, and relevant to the motion before the meeting.

No member may speak twice to the same question. A member may, however, reply to objections and make explanations; and the mover of a motion has the right to reply, but his speech in reply concludes the discussion.

No reply is admissible for the mover of a purely formal motion, such as adjournment, etc. The motion to which the privilege of reply is attached must be "substantive."

No speech can be made after the question has been put, and carried or negatived.

Any member may raise a point of order, it being understood that he rises "to order," but he must put the point concisely and without speech.

No speaker can "call" another to order. The chairman alone can properly do this. A member may, of course, rise to call the chairman's attention to "disorder," but the decision rests with the chair.

No question should be put to the vote so long as any member is desirous of speaking on it, or of moving an amendment to it, except in the special circumstances considered. (p. 66)

SECRETARIAL DUTIES.

These vary with the company or association in which the secretary is employed. He may be secretary to a Limited Company, a Hospital, or a Club.

All these have a basis of business which helps the official upon his way, but the details are different. The duties, therefore, of a secretary depend a good deal upon the nature of the society and its extent. In all companies the general duties of the secretary are:—

> To attend all the meetings (which he, moreover, has summoned) of company, directors, or even of committee if desired.
>
> To read the notice convening the meeting and the minutes of previous meeting.
>
> To keep the Agenda Book and the Minute Book of the company and directors' proceedings.
>
> To issue all notices to members, shareholders, directors, and in small societies to committee-men (of Clubs, etc.).
>
> To conduct or supervise all correspondence with the shareholders with regard to shares, transfers, etc., and general correspondence in many institutions.
>
> To keep the company's books, such as the Members' Register, Share Ledger, and Transfer Ledger.
>
> To make due and proper returns as required to the registrar of joint stock companies.

Besides such duties to the directors or committee of institutions or clubs, the secretary or hon. secretary has some social duties to perform in the way of welcoming guests and paying them little courtesies in the temporary absence of their hosts or friends. A good deal of the popularity of a club, particularly a small social club, will depend on the tact and *savoir faire* of the secretary. His duties will include the arrangement of the weekly or monthly dinners, the collection of the annual subscriptions, and the fees; the arrangement of any entertainments of the club or society; and the entertainment of club guests, etc. He will also call the committee together at certain periods, and keep a watchful eye upon the general arrangements of the club—the newspapers, stationery, pens and ink, and so on, so as to make all smooth as far as possible.

These are the general principles on which the secretary should work, and he should be able to prompt, and "coach" the chairman, if necessary, in the agenda and procedure (and the proceedings), of the meeting. He should at a dinner of the society be ready with all lists, and have the places marked, and, in fact, be social, pleasant, and generally useful.

APPENDIX B

Forms of Procedure and of Minutes for the use of Chairmen and Secretaries—Agenda.

I. Memoranda of procedure at meetings, when chairman is seated.

    (a) To call upon secretary to read the minutes of the last meeting.

    (b) To inquire if it is the wish of members that these minutes be signed as truly representing the facts of the previous meeting. If assent is given—

    (c) To sign the minutes.

    (d) To receive any motions which members may advance. To have them duly seconded, and to put them to the meeting in the prescribed form.

    (e) Either now or before the hearing of motions to go through the agenda paper placed before the chairman by secretary, and finish *routine* business.

[N.B.—This business is best concluded before any new motions by members are heard.]

    (f) Close meetings.

II. Memorandum of procedure when no chairman is appointed.

    (a) Proceed to elect chairman.

    (b) Chairman, when elected, to read notice convening the meeting, and announce its objects.

    (c) Proceed as per paragraph (d), and sequel, above.

    (d) Conclude and close meeting, or adjourn it.

N.B.—The agenda should contain all business. The agenda of the House of Commons are termed "The Orders of the Day."

III. Memorandum of procedure respecting the disposal of committee's report.

    (a) The committee having handed in the report to the chairman of the appointing body assembled in meeting, the chairman shall call upon the secretary to read the said report.

(b) The motion then should be made—the chairman should explain this—"that the report be 'received' or 'adopted'." In the former case (the reception), it is signified that the report is for the meeting; in the second case, the report is for publication.

(c) The motion should be seconded in the usual manner, and if the motion is agreed to, the next motion will be "That the report be entered in the minutes"; *or* "That" (if adopted) "the report be printed and published." Either of these motions, when made, must be seconded.

[There is no need to move the entry of an adopted report in the Minutes; that is done as a matter of course as a business transaction; but it is not absolutely a matter of course in the case of reception, though minutes are usually kept. In any case, whether it be or be not necessary to move the entry, the report must be recorded on the minutes.]

(d) Before the question is put "That the report be received" or "adopted," any member may move an amendment. Now is the time. Any objections, any suggestions for improvement or relegation to the committee, must be made now; and other members may be moved for—or even a new committee.